NEW DIRECTIONS
FOR
PHILANTHROPIC
FUNDRAISING

Robert E. Fogal
Ohio Presbyterian Retirement Services Foundation;
formerly of the Indiana University Center on Philanthropy
EDITOR-IN-CHIEF

ACHIEVING TRUSTEE INVOLVEMENT IN FUNDRAISING

Timothy L. Seiler
Indiana University
Kay Sprinkel Grace
San Francisco

EDITORS

NUMBER 4, SUMMER 1994

ACHIEVING TRUSTEE INVOLVEMENT IN FUNDRAISING
Timothy L. Seiler, Kay Sprinkel Grace (eds.)
New Directions for Philanthropic Fundraising, No. 4, Summer 1994
Robert E. Fogal, Editor-in-Chief

Microfilm copies of issues and articles are available in 16 mm and 35 mm, as well as microfiche in 105 mm, through University Microfilms Inc., 300 North Zeeb Road, Ann Arbor, Michigan 48106-1346.

ISSN 1072-172X   ISBN 0-7879-9970-9

NEW DIRECTIONS FOR PHILANTHROPIC FUNDRAISING is part of The Jossey-Bass Nonprofit Sector Series and is published quarterly by Jossey-Bass Inc., Publishers, 350 Sansome Street, San Francisco, California 94104-1310.

SUBSCRIPTIONS: Please see Ordering Information at back of book.

EDITORIAL CORRESPONDENCE should be sent to Robert E. Fogal, Ohio Presbyterian Retirement Services Foundation, OMNI Plaza, 4502 Darrow Rd., Rte. 91, Stow, OH 44224-1887.

Manufactured in the United States of America. Nearly all Jossey-Bass books, jackets, and periodicals are printed on recycled paper that contains at least 50 percent recycled waste, including 10 percent postconsumer waste. Many of our materials are also printed with vegetable-based ink; during the printing process these inks emit fewer volatile organic compounds (VOCs) than petroleum-based inks. VOCs contribute to the formation of smog.

Contents

Editor's Notes

THE CHAPTERS in this volume, *Achieving Trustee Involvement in Fundraising*, address diverse issues about trustees and fundraising and fit into four categories: historical perspectives on trusteeship, trustees and their roles, trustees and staff, and education of trustees. This range of approaches offers insights for trustees and for staff personnel who must tackle together the challenges facing today's not-for-profit organizations in raising the needed funds for carrying out their programs and fulfilling their missions.

Chapter One presents a historical perspective based on research into five settlement houses and their responses to the difficulties raised by the Great Depression. Paul H. Stuart argues that this historical view can be instructive in offering a model for trusteeship in our own difficult times today. Stuart maintains that in trying circumstances, the tendency to retreat into the familiar and the conventional is defeating, and innovative organizational behavior is a key to energizing organizational mission.

While Stuart's is the only chapter taking a historical view of trusteeship, the next two chapters address the fundamental issue of the role of trustees, particularly their responsibility for the fiscal health of their organizations and their nurturing of the vision of the organizations whose missions they advocate. In Chapter Two, Cheever Tyler, based on his personal experience as a trustee, maintains that a trustee's survival in today's fundraising environment calls for a reexamination of the fundamentals of trusteeship. Tyler offers a close look at three components that he defines as the basis for a survival strategy: excellence, access, and relevance of the service or product of the not-for-profit organization. He maintains that today's embattled trustee will not only survive but also succeed in attracting public support for the not-for-profit by leading the

NEW DIRECTIONS FOR PHILANTHROPIC FUNDRAISING, NO. 4, SUMMER 1994 © JOSSEY-BASS PUBLISHERS

organization to increasingly visionary roles reaching beyond the scope of the not-for-profit's traditional service area. His is an important look at the very basis on which not-for-profits function.

Lilya Wagner, in Chapter Three, constructs a model for developing a philanthropic attitude among board members that leads them and development professionals to a position of consensus on the why and how of fundraising. Wagner addresses three prevalent issues regarding board attitudes and development professionals' hopes and expectations of board participation in fundraising. Going beyond a description of the gap between perception and reality, she offers a workable model of successful cooperation between development practitioners and board members.

Wagner's chapter serves as a bridge from theory to practice by introducing the concept of trustees and staff interaction in fundraising. The next three chapters address the theme of the importance of close interaction between trustees and professional staff in successful fundraising. In Chapter Four, David La Piana presents a personal case history from his viewpoint as executive director of a not-for-profit mental health agency in Oakland, California. La Piana sketches three themes of a board-management culture that provides an orientation for trustees and staff: the effective differentiation of management and governance; the ability of trustees to view the agency as vital, potent, and developing; and the appropriate use of planning. La Piana observes that trustees generally are indispensable to the success of the not-for-profit yet forcefully makes the case that the executive director has ultimate responsibility for creating a culture that encourages board ownership and involvement in the organization. The conclusion of the chapter is a compelling illustration of how well this supportive culture works.

In Chapter Five, Eugene R. Tempel and I address the issue of building effective teams of trustees and professional development staff. Based on a series of interviews with senior-level major-gift fundraising staff and trustees of not-for-profits, we use the success stories of several organizations to construct a model for how staff and trustees can interact for successful fundraising. The chapter refers to several standards in fundraising literature to point out the lack of coverage of this topic in current fundraising literature. The interviews confirm what many trustees and professional development persons already know: There frequently are tensions between trustees and staff in carrying out the fundraising process. While the interviews reinforce conventional knowledge, they also offer insight into and confirmation of the reality of trustees and staff working together as compatible members of fundraising teams. Most important, the chapter outlines what trustees and staff expect of each other in the mutually respectful partnerships that lead to successful and rewarding fundraising. The chapter might be of special help for senior-level professionals in guiding their junior-level staff to increased comfort in their roles with trustees.

In Chapter Six, based on applied research, Winfred R. "Win" Winfree III cites data compiled from a questionnaire mailed to more than two hundred chief development officers at colleges and universities to look at the effective use of nondevelopment personnel in soliciting major gifts. The data reveal that nondevelopment personnel, defined as president or chancellor, board of trustees, private citizens, and faculty, played a significant role in soliciting more than half of the major gifts. Winfree ranks the effectiveness of each of the four groups in four steps of major-gift solicitation. While he concludes that certain attributes are less essential to fundraising success than is conventionally believed by senior development personnel, the data nevertheless confirm other strongly held beliefs about the role of nondevelopment personnel in fundraising. Winfree argues that there is a high potential for increased success in acquiring major gifts by effectively using these groups in major-gift activities.

In the final chapter, Santo D. Marabella, a college professor who also serves as manager of a leadership development program in Pennsylvania, offers concrete suggestions for a curriculum for educating and training effective trustees and directors of not-for-profit organizations. Basing his proposed curriculum on four major components central to preparing persons for board service, Marabella defines specific elements and identifies specific skills and issues of each component of the proposed course of study. The excitement generated by his chapter is the promise offered by a program designed to prepare boards of directors who are knowledgeable, competent, and confident voluntary leaders, capable of surviving and succeeding in the not-for-profit sector of the coming years.

In the Conclusion to this volume, Kay Sprinkel Grace highlights several thematic elements of these chapters. She focuses on one in particular as an instructive lesson from the volume: partnership. Grace contends that successful campaigns and organizations are characterized by mutual trust between boards and staff. She expands the concept by defining the key roles of staff and board, emphasizing that a successful partnership is fostered by clearly defined roles and expectations that are openly and honestly communicated. Successful partnerships are mutually reinforcing to boards and staff in discharging their responsibilities for the organization. Grace goes on to offer several insights into how this volume can be used by and useful to volunteers and paid staff in the third sector.

From a glance back in history to a look to the future, from the experience of a seasoned trustee to the perspective of a passionate executive director, with intervening attention to the theory and practice of successful board-staff interactions, these chapters cover a range of viewpoints centering on the topic of trustees and fundraising. The chapters offer a variety of reflections, observations, models, and prescriptions for trustees and staff to take seriously their role in securing financial resources for their not-for-profit organizations. They make a useful contribution to the work of trustees and staff in fulfilling their fundraising tasks.

Timothy L. Seiler
Editor

TIMOTHY L. SEILER *is director of Operations of the Fund Raising School, Indiana University Center on Philanthropy. He is formerly vice president of Indiana University Foundation in charge of its Indianapolis office.*

Settlement house leadership in the 1930s shares many characteristics with today's not-for-profits. The response of settlement house board members and executives to the crisis of the Great Depression suggests factors that contribute to innovation in voluntary social services organizations.

1

Trusteeship in difficult times: Settlement houses in the Great Depression

Paul H. Stuart

VOLUNTARY SOCIAL services agencies are today experiencing difficult times. As a result of federal and state budget cuts, disappointingly small increases in voluntary fundraising, and a failure to locate and tap new sources of financial support, discussions of "downsizing" and "cutback management" have increasingly characterized the literature of voluntary social services administration. Although "rightsizing," trimming unnecessary programs and eliminating waste, is a possible positive result of reductions in available funds, too often observers have noted a tendency to withdraw into the routine, into familiar and conventional activities, and to avoid innovation in difficult times (Drolen, 1990). Thus, when innovative organizational behavior is most needed, circumstances may frustrate the development of new ways of approaching organizational missions.

NEW DIRECTIONS FOR PHILANTHROPIC FUNDRAISING, NO. 4, SUMMER 1994 © JOSSEY-BASS PUBLISHERS

The response of the leaders of five settlement houses to the Great Depression of the 1930s is explored in this chapter. The administrative records of five settlement houses—Association House and Gads Hill Center of Chicago, the Baden Street Settlement of Rochester, New York, Denison House of Boston, and Kingsley House of New Orleans—provide the primary data for the study. In selecting settlement houses to investigate, I made an effort to avoid a reexamination of the better-known settlements, which have received extensive attention in the historical literature. Each settlement's staffing and use of volunteers, its sources of financing, and its record of innovation during the years between the end of World War I and the early 1960s were reviewed to illuminate the relationships among funding, use of volunteers, and innovation.

While the environment encountered by the voluntary social services during the Great Depression is not strictly analogous to that of our own time, there are striking parallels. During the 1930s, reductions in direct contributions and community chest allocations made it difficult for many settlement houses to maintain their normal programs, let alone innovate. Indeed, some community chests actively discouraged innovation, perhaps reinforcing the inclinations of professional and lay leaders. While the need for innovation had increased as the result of new social problems associated with the Depression, the need far exceeded the scope of new programs and services. Some new sources of support became available to settlement houses during the 1930s, but these were often structured in such a way as to make up for revenues lost as the result of the economic downturn, rather than make new initiatives possible. For the most part, new sources of support merely enabled settlements to maintain traditional programs.

However, some innovative programs were attempted, and the decade of the 1930s was not entirely devoid of change. Changes in board composition, in the responsibilities of board members, in settlement house financing, and in sources of staff and volunteers characterized the decade at a number of settlement houses.

Composition of boards

As is frequently the case with new organizations today, the ideal board member in the early years of the settlement movement was deeply involved in the day-to-day life of the settlement house. Board members often participated in the delivery of the settlement program directly to neighbors, as settlement house residents or as nonresident volunteers. Often, the board was elected by a settlement house association that included staff members and volunteers in its membership. Since the head resident and other paid staff members, as well as unpaid residents, often had the same social and educational backgrounds as those of board members, few distinctions were made among board members, staff members, and volunteers.

This changed by the 1930s when only a few of the older style patrician board members still served on settlement boards. Many board members were relatively uninvolved in the day-to-day work of the settlements. "The boards of directors [of settlement houses] seem very much like the governing boards of other private social work organizations," wrote Gaynell Hawkins (1937, p. 22). "They are for the most part well-intentioned, philanthropically inclined men and women who either have money of their own, or know where and how to get it, and share the same social interests as the settlements." However, according to settlement house board member Louise Klein (1937, pp. 2–3), board members were "not always people who are committed to settlement work." Their "interest fluctuates as does their value." Many served "on too many boards" and resented "demands made upon their time."

As a result of the changing composition of boards, settlement leaders increasingly emphasized the selection of board members. Ruth Austin, the head resident of Gads Hill Center, wrote (n.d. [c. 1940], p. 1) that "auxiliaries in one form or another can be used as proving grounds from which new Board members can be selected." She recruited as board members persons who had volunteered at the settlement, often as part of service club projects.

Since a major function of settlements was to promote mutual understanding between rich and poor, some advocated including neighborhood residents on boards of directors. Indeed, Farra (1931) found that over one-fourth of New York City settlements (nine out of thirty-four) had neighborhood residents on their boards. At least one additional New York settlement had eliminated neighborhood representation on the governing board in favor of persons who could contribute financially.

In other cities, neighborhood representation on the governing board was less likely than in New York. Few neighborhood residents served on settlement house boards in Minneapolis in the 1930s (Karger, 1987). Hawkins (1937) was disappointed to find relatively little neighborhood representation on governing boards.

In general, settlement house board members represented the well-off business and professional classes. Settlement house workers and head residents were increasingly from the ranks of career workers with professional aspirations, whether or not they had been professionally educated. Despite the settlement ideology of serving as a bridge across social classes, relatively few Depression-era board members or settlement house workers came from settlement house neighborhoods.

Responsibilities of board members

Some aspects of the board member's role during the Depression were relatively unchanged. As in earlier decades, board members were expected to ensure the settlement's financial survival. Farra (1931, p. 4) found that, in New York City, "membership on a settlement board practically always implies financial responsibility." Participation in the community chest, which might have been expected to relieve board members of this responsibility, did not in fact do so. In community chest cities, board members were expected to work in the annual fundraising campaigns.

However, there was less clarity regarding the board member's role beyond his or her financial responsibility. In part, this result-ed from the increasing specialization of all social services agencies, including settlement houses, and the consequent emphasis on trained expertise in social services, which left some board members uncertain about their roles. "Certainly we are good for something more" than raising money, wrote board member Sidney Hollander (1939, p. 550). He concluded that board members had a responsi-bility to ensure that agency services were needed, that the services provided by the agency could not otherwise be met, and that the services were being effectively performed.

Commonly, board members were expected to interpret the needs of the settlement movement in relation to the larger community. "The all the year round job for each [board] member is to interpret to the community not only University House, but equally the phi-losophy of the settlement movement," wrote Benjamin West Frazier (1936, p. 1), the president of a Philadelphia settlement house. "This I believe to be the prime contribution of any board member" (p. 2). To enable the board to perform this function, Frazier tried "to make our board meetings . . . a training course for the members."

Other settlements attempted to educate board members by in-volving them in particular projects at the settlement houses or by providing special educational programs for them. For example, Klein (1937) reported that the Detroit Federation of Settlements provided a monthly program for representatives of settlement boards; one Detroit settlement provided an educational program, led by the head resident, for board members, complete with read-ing assignments and field trips.

In assuming an educational stance toward board members, head residents and other staff reflected a basic change in the board and staff composition of settlement houses that occurred during the previous decade. As staff members were more likely to differ from board members in social background, they were more likely to em-phasize their superior experience and expertise. Board members, who increasingly were busy people with a variety of interests not related to the settlement houses, were more likely to accept the role of learner. In part, the emphasis on the expertise of the staff reflected the bureaucratization and professionalization of the social agency during the 1920s, a process that Lubove (1965, pp. 218–219) found was accelerated by participation in federated fundraising organizations. Board member Sidney Hollander (1939) called for intensive training of social agency board members by professional staff members. This emphasis on training probably enhanced the power of staff members to influence voluntary agency policy. As Ralph Kramer (1965) pointed out, educational programs for governing board members may serve to diminish ideological differences between the board and social agency executives. The result, he suggested, may be that "the executive exerts a greater influence than the board member in the policy process" (p. 114) in the voluntary social agency.

Financing

During the first decades of the twentieth century, most settlement houses survived on the contributions of small groups of interested friends, who either pledged annual contributions (often called subscriptions or dues) or committed themselves to make up any deficit in the houses' operating budgets. Often, the settlement executive, called the head resident, was one of this group, and in a few settlements these executives provided significant portions of the financing. A number of settlements were supported by religious denominations, and a smaller number received income from endowments. Some settlements attempted to raise money from appeals to the general public, but these appeals often fell short of expectations. The predominant method of financing settlements prior to the 1920s was reliance on small groups of patrons or donors.

During World War I, a number of cities organized federated fundraising campaigns to support war-related charities, such as the Red Cross. Settlement houses that provided war-related services participated in these drives, and each received a share of the proceeds. After the war, these war chests were reorganized as community chests, designed to support the voluntary social services agencies of the community. Although many in the settlement movement viewed federated fundraising as a threat to the settlements' traditional flexibility because of the chests' commitment to "stereotyped forms of social work" (Cooper, 1923, p. 24), participation in federated fundraising campaigns became a popular means of settlement financing during the 1920s.

Baden Street Settlement joined Rochester's Community and Patriotic Fund, the wartime name of that city's community chest, in 1918, making it one of the first settlements in the nation to participate in federated fundraising. Denison House and Kingsley House affiliated with the community chests in Boston and New Orleans, respectively, during the 1920s. Each of these three settlements quickly came to depend on community chest allocations. By 1922, Baden Street Settlement was "dependent largely on the Community Chest" (Adler, 1922). In all three cases, membership served to maintain, but not to expand, settlement house programs. Indeed, none of the three settlements developed significant new programs during the decade. While participation in the community chests represented a loss of autonomy for settlement houses, it also presented financial advantages. Allocations from the community chests tended to be relatively reliable from year to year. Community chest allocations usually represented a significant proportion of each participating settlement house's annual budget. Reliance on a small group of friends, patrons, and large contributors, on the other hand, often resulted in a budget that fluctuated widely from year to year. While one year's community chest allocation might have been more or less than the prior year's, the fluctuation was not large and the approximate size of the agency's annual budget tended to be more predictable. This stability made it possible for settlement houses to achieve consistency in staffing patterns and to establish regular ongoing programs.

Community chest membership provided settlement houses with the additional benefit of participation in planned communitywide campaigns for social welfare services. Most community chests funded a council of social agencies that had the responsibility for communitywide social planning. Thus, by participating in the campaign and social planning activities of the community chest, a settlement house could participate in a communitywide activity with a high level of legitimacy and at the same time potentially influence community social welfare planning. Councils of social agencies sometimes provided an impetus for agency innovation. They became particularly important during the early 1930s, as voluntary agencies took the lead in attempting to respond to the crises of the Depression.

Only Chicago and New York, among large American cities, resisted the trend toward federated fundraising during the 1920s. Voluntary agencies in these two largest American cities were able to find sufficient support without participation in community chests. During the Depression, however, social services agencies in both cities experienced reductions in contributions. Both cities established federated fundraising mechanisms during the 1930s. Nearly all settlement houses participated in federated fundraising campaigns by the mid 1930s.

Both Association House and Gads Hill Center joined the Chicago Community Fund, organized in 1934. Gads Hill Center's budget was "very much curtailed" during the early years of the Depression (Gads Hill Center, 1934). In February 1934, the Gads Hill board voted to join a proposed community fund, conditioned on the participation of all other Chicago social agencies, a sympathetic view by the fund toward social settlements, and a commitment to increase the Gads Hill budget "when general conditions improved" (Gads Hill Center, 1934).

Unlike the situation in Boston, Rochester, and New Orleans, the fiscal impact of membership in the Chicago Community Fund was relatively limited. Community fund allocations were designed to supplement the member agency's regular fundraising efforts and accounted for only 30 to 40 percent of the Association House budget during the 1930s (Association House, 1939). At Gads Hill Center, community fund allocations accounted for 20 to 35 percent of the agency's annual budget between 1934 and 1940, while contributions from individuals and organizations accounted for a slightly larger proportion of the budget (Gads Hill Center, 1930–1940). Because of the smaller financial contribution, as compared to community chests, the impact of the Chicago Community Fund on settlement house programming was limited as well. New York and Chicago settlement houses maintained their independence by securing sufficient funds to operate, if at a reduced level, independently. Some settlement houses in these cities provided innovative programs during the 1930s.

New sources of staff and volunteers

The Depression of the 1930s created increased demands for the recreational services provided by many settlement houses, since unemployed adults had more leisure time. The Depression also caused a resurgence of volunteering. Settlements needed volunteers because of reductions in direct contributions as well as community chest allocations. Unemployed persons volunteered at settlements in order to build records of voluntary service as a way of increasing their employment prospects (Jones, 1968; Jones and Herrick, 1976). Settlement leaders emphasized the need for "careful training and ongoing direction" of volunteers. The new volunteers were extremely valuable, but some settlement houses experienced difficulties with volunteer workers. Most of these difficulties were attributed to "problems of poor supervision." The "most successful volunteers" were "students in training"—social work, education, or recreation students receiving academic credit for field education ("Volunteers," 1936; Committee on Volunteers, 1940).

Two New Deal work relief programs, the Works Progress Administration (WPA) and the National Youth Administration (NYA), provided paid workers who helped to maintain settlement house programming at pre-Depression levels. These workers took the place of employees who had been laid off due to budget cuts and, at some settlements, replaced volunteers as well. In many cases, WPA and NYA workers were essential for settlement houses to maintain even minimal programs (Peterson, 1965; Trolander, 1975). Much of the recreation program provided by Association House, for example, was supervised by personnel supplied by WPA. When WPA enrollments were cut in the early 1940s, it was difficult for the settlement to maintain its recreation program (Association House, 1941).

The influx of new volunteers and work relief personnel served to maintain, rather than change, settlement house programming. In part, this was because the new resources came at a time when the funds available to the settlements were being reduced. It made sense to utilize these new workers to carry on an existing program that was threatened. Also, the administrators of the work relief programs were not concerned about the innovativeness of the settlements; their intent was to put unemployed people to work. Thus, there was no incentive for settlement houses to innovate.

New relations with public programs

Before World War I, a major function of settlement houses had been to develop new programs and demonstrate their usefulness. Following a successful demonstration, settlement personnel and their allies would campaign to have the new programs taken over by the city or state government or by a specialized private agency. Examples include antituberculosis measures, occupational health programs, maternal and child health programs, legal aid services, and vocational guidance services (Addams, 1931). With the involvement of most settlement houses in the community chest movement, this settlement function was much curtailed during the 1920s. Settlement leaders, however, still liked to think of themselves as urban pioneers, running "experiment-stations in social work" (White, 1911, p. 62).

Despite this tradition, the relationship between public and private social services became a vexing problem during the Depression as public responsibility for social services increased. A movement "to unload certain forms of social work on public authority" (National Federation of Settlements, n.d. [c. 1928]) began in the late 1920s. Municipal governments in the United States varied greatly in the social, health, and recreational services that they provided. Community chests, in response to steady or declining contributions, promoted municipal assumption of what had been voluntary philanthropic activities.

The recreational emphasis developed by the settlement movement in the 1920s placed some settlement houses in a difficult position as pressures grew for municipal governments to expand public recreation programs. "The chest people are going after the proposition of unloading what they can on the city and the state," wrote a settlement leader after attending a community chest conference in 1928. "We cannot possibly afford to quarrel with this particular motive which is a traditional settlement one. We always have called ourselves experiment stations, denied any intention to build up an institution and agreed that when forms of work have been demonstrated they might very well be turned over to either public or private sponsors. I am not at all sure that the settlements would not do well to accept the challenge of this point of view in a very broad way and unite to see what can be done to foster the growth of all kinds of municipal education and recreation" (National Federation of Settlements, n.d. [c. 1928]). The most likely candidate for a new focus for the settlements seemed to be adult education.

The crisis of the Depression frustrated efforts to expand municipal services. The provision of relief to the unemployed by public and private agencies met a more pressing need. Providing relief was an important function for many voluntary agencies during the early years of the Depression, sometimes with city or state subsidies. When the new Roosevelt administration set up the Federal Emergency Relief Administration in 1933, however, subsidies to voluntary agencies for relief giving were prohibited. All public relief was to be provided by public agencies. Voluntary agencies were required to define functions that did not duplicate those provided by government agencies (Swift, 1934).

Five settlements during the Great Depression

The five settlements whose programs are reviewed above did not alter their programs greatly during the 1930s. For the most part, despite a few attempts to respond to emergencies, the programs that had been developed in the past were maintained by the five settlement houses during the 1930s.

At Gads Hill Center, the staff attempted to respond to Depression-era emergencies, in addition to carrying on the program that the settlement had developed over the past three decades. In the early 1930s, the staff coped with "after five o'clock emergencies," distribution of emergency relief, homelessness, and lack of jobs for young people. By the middle of the decade, however, discussion of new Depression-related programs at Gads Hill ceased, perhaps because the development of New Deal relief programs provided sources of help to which clients could be referred. By the late 1930s, Gads Hill emphasized a traditional settlement house program of clubs and classes, together with a number of programs that were begun in the 1920s, such as a music school and a nursery school. Gads Hill also provided space for a branch library and a neighborhood office for the visiting nurses association. The size of the staff remained relatively constant during the 1930s, with nine or ten full-time workers, three to five part-time workers, three to six resident volunteers, and five to eleven nonresident volunteers (Gads Hill Center, 1930–1940).

During the 1930s, Association House, which was sponsored by the Presbyterian Church, emphasized youth and adult recreation. The settlement's neighborhood was largely Polish and Catholic. Some religious programming was provided, but it was not emphasized. Four

Four Sunday School classes and one vesper service were provided per week. In contrast, in a typical week, the settlement conducted forty-one adult and thirty-two children's classes, twenty-two children's club meetings, twenty-two gym periods, eleven game room periods, nine dance classes, and smaller numbers of other recreational and educational activities (Association House, 1937).

The Rochester Community Chest supported the Baden Street Settlement's prewar program during the 1920s. Even during that prosperous decade, the "most rigid economies" were demanded, and funding for expansions in the settlement's program was not provided (Social Settlement of Rochester, 1922; Michaels and Michaels, 1926). During the Depression, community chest allocations were reduced; the settlement cut its budget, and the board of directors increased its contributions to maintain a minimal program (Baden Street Settlement Treasurer, 1931).

At Kingsley House, program stagnation resulted from an aging leadership during the 1920s and 1930s. Kingsley House moved into new, donated quarters in 1924; ten years later, Eleanor McMain, head resident since 1901, died after a long illness. During the rest of the 1930s, the settlement maintained a program that differed little from that of earlier years and that served a declining number of neighbors. Early in the next decade, the New Orleans Council of Social Agencies helped Kingsley House respond to its problems. The council helped Kingsley House restructure its board of directors. A new head resident, Emeric Kurtagh, was hired in 1941. Kurtagh, a professional social worker, had directed an innovative adult education program at New York's Henry Street Settlement. He embarked on a program "of greater scope and quality than anything undertaken in the past," in the words of Ferguson Colcock (1941), the president of the Kingsley House Association.

Denison House's program focused increasingly on youth recreation during the 1920s. As the former neighborhood residents, Italians, Greeks, and Syrians, moved out of the neighborhood during the 1930s, the settlement increasingly served former neighbors who returned to the neighborhood only to participate in its programs.

An increasingly smaller proportion of neighborhood residents participated in Denison House programs. In part, this reflected the conversion of residential property into commercial property in the settlement's neighborhood, just south of Boston's downtown. In addition, settlement staff had difficulty relating to their new neighbors, Chinese immigrants. With encouragement from the community chest, Denison House initiated a move from Boston's South End to the Dorchester-Roxbury neighborhood in 1941. While the move took over a decade to complete, Denison House was providing some services in its new neighborhood by the summer of 1942 (Denison House, 1942; Hudson, n.d. [c. 1942]).

Conclusion

"Children and sickness are the keys that unlock most pocketbooks," wrote adult educator Gaynell Hawkins (1937, pp. 21–22); settlements were expected "to hold fast to those parts of its [*sic*] program that bring money." Indeed, recreation and health programs, especially maternal and child health programs, were important at many settlement houses. Recreation programs for children were nearly universal. In the 1930s, as afterward, community chests allocated funds to agencies organized in functional areas; settlement houses were placed in the group work and recreation section in most cities. Both structural and fundraising considerations discouraged innovation; maintaining existing programs seemed enough of an accomplishment during the 1930s.

This finding is consistent with the conclusions of others who have examined settlement houses during the Great Depression. Trolander (1975) contrasted the Depression experience of the settlements with the 1960s, a decade marked by much more programmatic innovation. Karger (1987, pp. 86–87) found that Minneapolis settlement houses "changed remarkably little" during the 1930s. Their response to the crisis of the Great Depression was, in his words, "more of the same."

What do these case histories suggest for today's trustees? While there are many differences between the 1930s and the 1990s, both were periods of serious resource constraint for voluntary social services organizations. Since World War II, government resources, in the forms of contracts, grants, subsidies, and fees for services, have become much more important for these organizations than was previously the case (Stuart, 1992). It is the crisis in government budgets, rather than an economic depression, that has created problems for voluntary agencies today. Still, as resources are found to support voluntary agencies, trustees and directors will be responsive to the way in which access to these resources is structured. It is probable that the trusteeship function is inherently conservative. Trustees, after all, are responsible for ensuring the survival of the organizations that have been entrusted to their care. When innovation is a condition for acquiring new resources, as was the case briefly during the 1960s, innovation will be widespread. However, when resources are available to carry on business as usual, as was the case during the 1930s, innovation will be rare. However, even during the 1930s, some settlement houses did develop innovative programs to confront the problems of the Great Depression. Among the most successful were settlement houses located in New York and Chicago, where federated fundraising contributed about half of what was contributed to agency budgets in other cities. This suggests that overreliance on a single source of revenue may stifle innovation. Sensitive leadership is important, as well. The challenge for our own times is twofold: to structure opportunities for new resources for voluntary organizations that foster innovation and to foster sensitivity to emerging community needs among trustees and executives.

References

Addams, J. "Social Workers and the Other Professions." In *Proceedings of the National Conference of Social Work, 1930.* Chicago: University of Chicago Press, 1931.

Adler, I. "Letter to Mrs. J. L. Garson, Rochester, N.Y., Feb. 17, 1922." In

Baden Street Settlement Records, box 3, folder 36, Social Welfare History Archives, University of Minnesota, Minneapolis, 1922.

Association House. "Service Report." In *Association House Records*, box 7, folder 6, Chicago Historical Society, 1937.

Association House. "Community Fund Budget Report." In *Association House Records*, box 7, folder 9, Chicago Historical Society, 1939.

Association House. "Service Report." *Association House Records*, box 7, folder 6, Chicago Historical Society, 1941.

Austin, R. "Report of Institute on Settlement Administration, Interpretation, and Development of Relationships Between Boards, Staff, and Neighbors." In *National Federation of Settlements Records*, New York, box 11, folder 87, Social Welfare History Archives, University of Minnesota, Minneapolis, n.d. (c. 1940).

Baden Street Settlement Treasurer. "Letter to Harry H. Stebbins, Chairman, Budget Committee, Rochester Community Chest, Rochester, N.Y., June 2, 1931." In *Baden Street Settlement Records*, box 7, folder 87, Social Welfare History Archives, University of Minnesota, Minneapolis, 1931.

Colcock, F. "Letters to Community Chest Budget Committee, New Orleans, Dec. 1, 1941, and Dec. 16, 1941 (Revision of Letter of Dec. 1, 1941)." In *Kingsley House Papers*, box 7, folder 30, Howard-Tilton Memorial Library, Tulane University, New Orleans, 1941.

Committee on Volunteers. "Volunteers." *Round Table*, 1940, 5 (1), 4–6.

Cooper, C. C. *Settlement Finance*. Boston: National Federation of Settlements, 1923.

Denison House. "Denison House in Transition: Organization and Program for 1942." In *Denison House Records*, box 4, folder 20, Schlesinger Library, Radcliffe College, Cambridge, Mass., 1942.

Drolen, C. S. "Current Community Mental Health Center Operations: Entrepreneurship or Business as Usual?" *Community Mental Health Journal*, 1990, *26* (6), 547–558.

Farra, K. "The Organization and Administration of New York Settlements." In *National Federation of Settlements Records*, New York, box 51, folder 537, Social Welfare History Archives, University of Minnesota, Minneapolis, 1931.

Frazier, B. W. "Experiences of a Settlement Board Member." In *National Federation of Settlements Records*, box 10, folder 82, Social Welfare History Archives, University of Minnesota, Minneapolis, 1936.

Gads Hill Center. "Annual Reports, 1930–1940." In *National Federation of Settlements Records*, Chicago, box 30, folder 289, Social Welfare History Archives, University of Minnesota, Minneapolis, 1930–1940.

Gads Hill Center. "Board of Trustees Minutes, Feb. 9, 1934." In *Gads Hill Center Records*, box 1, folder 5, Chicago Historical Society, 1934.

Hawkins, G. *Educational Experiences in Social Settlements*. New York: American Association for Adult Education, 1937.

Hollander, S. "Confessions of a Board Member." In *Proceedings of the National Conference of Social Work, 1939*. New York: Columbia University Press, 1939.

Hudson, E. W. "Report on Denison House." In *Denison House Records*, box 5, folder 26, Schlesinger Library, Radcliffe College, Cambridge, Mass., n.d. (c. 1942).

Jones, J. F. "The Use of Volunteers in American Social Welfare During the Depression." Unpublished doctoral dissertation, School of Social Work, University of Minnesota, 1968.

Jones, J. F., and Herrick, J. M. *Citizens in Service: Volunteers in Social Welfare During the Depression, 1929–1941*. East Lansing: Michigan State University Press, 1976.

Karger, H. J. *The Sentinels of Order: A Study of Social Control and the Minneapolis Settlement House Movement, 1915–1950*. Lanham, Md.: University Presses of America, 1987.

Klein, L. F. "Conference of the National Federation of Settlements, Board Member Division, May 20, 1937." In *National Federation of Settlements Records*, New York, box 10, folder 83, Social Welfare History Archives, University of Minnesota, Minneapolis, 1937.

Kramer, R. M. "Ideology, Status, and Power in Board-Executive Relationships." *Social Work*, 1965, *10* (4), 107–114.

Lubove, R. *The Professional Altruist: The Emergence of Social Work as a Career, 1880–1930*. Cambridge, Mass.: Harvard University Press, 1965.

Michaels, J., and Michaels, Mrs. J. "Letter to Mrs. J. L. Garson, Rochester, N.Y., Nov. 30, 1926." In *Baden Street Settlement Records*, box 7, folder 87, Social Welfare History Archives, University of Minnesota, Minneapolis, 1926.

National Federation of Settlements. "Transcript of a Letter from the Secretary to the President." In *National Federation of Settlements Records*, box 13, folder 100, Social Welfare History Archives, University of Minnesota, Minneapolis, n.d. (c. 1928).

Peterson, J. A. "From Social Settlement to Social Agency: Settlement Work in Columbus, Ohio, 1898–1958." *Social Service Review*, 1965, *39* (2), 191–208.

Social Settlement of Rochester. "Treasurer's Report." In *Baden Street Settlement Records*, Rochester, N.Y., box 7, folder 86, Social Welfare History Archives, University of Minnesota, Minneapolis, 1922.

Stuart, P. H. *Philanthropy, Voluntarism, and Innovation: Settlement Houses in Twentieth-Century America*. Essays on Philanthropy, no. 5. Indianapolis: Indiana University Center on Philanthropy, 1992.

Swift, L. B. *New Alignments Between Public and Private Agencies*. New York: Family Welfare Association, 1934.

Trolander, J. *Settlement Houses and the Great Depression*. Detroit, Mich.: Wayne State University Press, 1975.

"Volunteers." *Round Table*, 1936, *1* (1), 1–8.

White, G. S. "The Social Settlement After Twenty-Five Years." *Harvard Theological Review*, 1911, *4*, 47–70.

PAUL H. STUART *is professor at the School of Social Work, University of Alabama, Tuscaloosa.*

Trustees will be the principal designers of survival strategies in this decade and will need to look beyond traditional alternatives in order to succeed.

2

Trusteeship, vision, and fundraising: Return to the fundamentals

Cheever Tyler

TRUSTEES who accept board positions in the nonprofit sector today will be faced with astonishing challenges, particularly where the task of raising funds is concerned. Those who are willing to accept these challenges will need vision and a clear grasp of the fundamentals of nonprofit trusteeship to do the job well.

We are in an environment in which the growing sophistication of nonprofit organizations has made the hunt for financial support more sporting than ever before. In addition, trends that have been emerging for the last few years have now become permanent parts of the landscape, making fundraising harder to do.

For example, corporate grantmakers are looking more than ever before for giving opportunities that fit within their marketing strategies, or that answer some other corporate need. Corporate philanthropy is increasingly being viewed as an investment; and, as a result, grant requests are being scrutinized with an eye to the objectives of the corporate grantmaker. The trustee should be aware of the basic premise that has begun to define corporate philanthropy: Corporate philanthropy must be good for the shareholders. Fortunately,

NEW DIRECTIONS FOR PHILANTHROPIC FUNDRAISING, NO. 4, SUMMER 1994 © JOSSEY-BASS PUBLISHERS

most enlightened corporate managers acknowledge that companies are also in business for the good of the public, and if the public benefits, so too do the shareholders. Many managers, however, need to be persuaded.

Next, as government is cutting back everywhere, the nonprofit sector is being asked, as always, to step in. This only increases the number of nonprofits looking for funding, without a matching increase in the availability of funds.

We are also seeing how fragile the nonprofit world can be. The management tragedy at the United Way of America has illuminated an emerging skepticism of the integrity of the nonprofit sector. While the United Way incident may appear to be isolated, we will find that a little skepticism goes a long way. Just a few stories about personal benefit from charitable enterprises already have done a great deal of damage to the credibility of the nonprofit enterprise and, as in the case of the United Way, will result in predictable and substantial long-term decreases in public support. A by-product is that the public is demanding not only that the nonprofit sector provide honest administration but also that the services provided genuinely contribute to the public interest.

A newer but significant factor is that sophisticated grantmakers, particularly in urban areas, recognize that the complexity of urban problems requires multidimensional solutions. These grantmakers are looking for programs that have a broad community context and linkages to other efforts. They have learned that their grant funds are best used when they are leveraged by collaborative work across agencies.

Added to this factor is clear and convincing demographic evidence that by the turn of the century, or shortly thereafter, a majority of Americans will be members of minority groups who have not always had the easiest access to the arts, health care, and educational or social services. Members of these groups have achieved a certain degree of parity in political situations, but not in economic ones. If this trend continues, our economic apparatus will come into conflict with our political infrastructure, particularly in the urban centers where tensions are already high. This issue presents a challenge. Urban grantmakers are eager to resolve this problem and are looking to the nonprofit sector for help.

On this stage stands the trustee. These characteristics are the scenery on that stage. The trustee is charged with the obligation of finding money for his or her organization to function, and to provide badly needed services at a time when resources are scarce, while demand and competition are both growing. The trustee is the architect of the organization's plan to market itself to funding sources. The obligation to design a survival strategy rests squarely on the shoulders of the trustee, and it must be shouldered in a difficult and sometimes inhospitable climate. Now is a time for a reexamination of the fundamental elements of trusteeship—in effect, we must take the concept of trusteeship apart so that the whole can be better understood.

A significant and highly desirable element of good trusteeship is vision. The trustee should know the capabilities of the organization as well as its limitations. Above all, however, the trustee should know the community, and the people who will be asked to give. This vantage point, a higher ground, should permit the trustee a vision that incorporates a view of the close-up issues as well as of priorities and opportunities within the institution's more distant environment. How trustees make use of the view from the high ground will shape the institution's mission and policies and determine whether the organization will survive in the current climate and that of the future.

Vision involves a capacity to understand why the organization exists, with a clear and unambiguous understanding of the constituency served and of the needs that the organization can and cannot realistically address. Vision is the ability to see the community as a whole, and to understand how linkages among service organizations, corporate and individual donors, and foundations can be forged to expand the contribution of the nonprofit sector. Vision involves sophisticated networking not only on a communitywide basis but also within states and regions to attract support, and to recognize opportunity.

The visionary trustee must find ways to show that the services provided by the nonprofit sector are so valuable that they invite the necessary investment at a time when other pressing demands are being made on the pocketbooks of patrons. If the institution is a critical part of the quality of life in its community, it will be supported because most people agree that someone needs to do the job of caring for and nurturing the community. Trustees are doing their jobs when the community can truthfully say that if the organization were not there, it would need to be invented. The trick is how to accomplish this task. Here are several concepts that may be helpful.

Public benefit

At first blush, an opera company is there to sing, a college is there to teach, and a hospital is there to provide inpatient and outpatient health care services. A theater is there to put on shows, and a United Way is there to gather up money and give it away. Remember, however, that those who supported these efforts were able to deduct their gifts for federal and possibly state tax purposes. This means that fewer tax dollars were raised, with the result that every taxpayer in theory paid something to make it possible for the opera company to sing. Of course, the economics of tax policy are more complex than that, but however argued, the government and the giving public expect tax-exempt organizations to serve broadly public purposes. The notion of public purpose and service is critical to the issue of vision. It is always useful to ask how the nonprofit organization can do the most good for the largest number of people.

The public and the sophisticated grantmaker, whether corporate or not, understand that the community has the burden of self-help. The more each organization can help relieve that burden in creative and relevant ways, the more it is likely to be supported.

In the case of any organization, excellence, accessibility, relevance, and linkage offer a high form of public service. As a result, these are fundamental qualities of vision.

Quality

Trustees must have in mind that high standards of quality in the delivery of service will be rewarded by grantmakers. High quality is most likely to enrich audiences, most likely to heal in the case of the hospital, and most likely to reach the greatest number of beneficiaries in the case of the United Way and its agencies. In the case of education institutions, the competition for tuition-paying students will be won only by the best schools. Attaining quality, particularly at an economic cost to the nonprofit enterprise, takes vision and courage on the part of trustees, who will be charged with the responsibility of raising the funds to make it possible for the highest level of quality to be achieved. It takes a deliberate fundraising commitment in most cases to be the best. The Saint Louis Symphony and the San Francisco Ballet Association, for instance, decided that excellence was the way to grow. As a result of a financial commitment by their boards, who rallied their communities in turn, the symphony and the ballet have each achieved their goal of excellence and widespread public applause. There is no doubt that quality of service is among the best characteristics an enterprise can have when it is time to ask for money. Excellence is not a new concept, of course. But it clearly is a strategy for survival.

Access

A highly relevant and fundamental element of a nonprofit's public mission is broad accessibility to the organization's program of services. The task of providing access is often difficult, as in the case of a performing arts company or a college or university, where the cost of providing the service is high and the need for fee-for-service income often drives the "sticker price" beyond the reach of those who might most benefit from the services provided.

Health care institutions need to continue to design outreach programs that work. In New Haven and elsewhere where the problems of infant mortality and low birth weight are so staggering, and young pregnant mothers are not in the habit of seeing doctors, hospitals have created mobile units that travel to the neighborhoods to deliver care to the children having children in the communities served.

Some arts organizations, as well as health care providers, have sought means to bring their services into the schools. In the case of the arts, the trustees of the Shubert Performing Arts Center in New Haven, aware of their responsibility to ensure that the broadest possible audience is enriched by the center's art, raise funds annually to finance Project Access, whereby prime tickets are made available to disadvantaged beneficiaries of United Way agencies, usually single-parent families unable to pay for admission at normal prices. Other tickets are routinely given to nursing homes and social services agencies. At the Shubert, corporate sponsors are also asked to "buy down" the prices of tickets to attractions of interest to minority communities, so as to provide access at affordable prices. In such a case, a sponsor with a consumer product or service, such as a retail bank, pays a sponsorship fee that is used to relieve the theater of the need to charge high prices for tickets to the event or series of events. In a recent case, this approach made it possible for the theater to sell every seat in the house for a Latino dance festival for $5, where the average price without sponsorship would have approached $20.

In the field of higher education, the problem of accessibility is more difficult. Faced with an awareness of their responsibility to the minority community, many colleges have admitted students widely disparate in their levels of preparedness in order to make the campuses demographically representative and have preferred minorities in hiring decisions. Furthermore, these colleges have provided "racially or ethnically exclusive financial aid and academic counseling programs, as well as special administration, ombudsmen and resource centers to serve the putative representatives of selected student groups." While the National Association of Scholars admits that these practices, and others intended to attract minority students and to integrate them as quickly as possible, were generally "well-intentioned," they argue that these undertakings have resulted instead in intergroup tension in these colleges, without fully achieving the desired ends. Whatever the merits of the arguments presented, it is nonetheless clear that trustees of public as well as private colleges and universities must strive now, more than ever before, to find ways in which to integrate minority students into the mainstream of our economy, and to raise the funds to do so.

There seems to be no doubt that grantmakers looking to invest their shrinking charitable budgets in areas where the return will be the most dramatic prefer those organizations that provide a wide opportunity for public access. This makes extremely good business sense for the donor, and good business sense for the nonprofit grantee. The truly visionary trustee thinks of ways to provide broad public access as a strategy for survival. The task is essentially a planning and fundraising challenge, which is where the trustees come in.

Linkage and leverage

Most nonprofits are institutions that satisfy existing public needs with competent professional staff and well-meaning, energetic volunteers. That puts them in a unique position to effect change, particularly in cooperation with other organizations similarly inclined. In order to provide critical services, it makes sense to link existing organizations and programs to reduce duplication where it exists, and, more important, to provide linkage or leverage that permits a dollar invested to do two or three jobs rather than just one. This sort of leverage pleases grantmakers.

For example, the trustees of the New Haven Public Education Fund and the Shubert Performing Arts Center discovered two years ago that there were no libraries in the lower public schools in New Haven. Those trustees also discovered, after some basic research, that very few students in these schools had books of their own to enjoy. Understanding that an ability to read and a love of literature are central to a student's access to the "lifeboat" away from poverty, the trustees embarked on the Spotlight for Books program. The Shubert, as a full partner in the venture with the Public Education Fund, invited every playgoer who came to "Les Miserables" at the Shubert over a three-week period to bring a book for these children. The effort produced over ten thousand books of high quality in the first year of the program. With the help of librarians from Yale and the New Haven school system, the books were catalogued and placed in service. In the second year of the program, a like number of books were collected and distributed to lower-school students who were invited to attend a performance at the Shubert in which entertainers spoke to them about summer programs and the avoidance of the drug culture. In these situations, the theater used its institutional influence and strengths in combination with other nonprofits to help address an unrelated but vital problem.

Again in New Haven, the trustees of the New Haven Foundation several years ago saw a reduction in available private funds for the arts and began the Arts Challenge program. In this case, arts organizations were asked to find new donors, and to turn the new money raised over to the foundation to be placed into a permanent trust for the arts. The foundation, in turn, gave $1.50 to each arts organization for every $1.00 turned over to the permanent trust, to be used by the arts organization for current operating purposes. This matching program attracted new money with astonishing success. The program has attracted well over $1 million in trust funds, with the result that the program could well run itself from the investment income earned by the trust. A substantially higher number of gifts have been given to the arts than would otherwise have been given, and new donors and new audiences have been developed as well.

In the case of colleges and universities, leadership and the sharing of the enormous resources at hand in connection with community projects involving other community enterprises are vital. Whether in the form of providing educational opportunities to community residents, technical assistance to other organizations, or financial aid, the personal involvement of the college's or university's leadership is critical. Colleges and universities that depend on the largesse of the communities in which their campuses are located as well as on the gifts of educated and aware graduates must recognize the force of their presence within their communities and use that influence and their resources appropriately to lead, to convene, and to help the communities survive at all levels by working with other elements of the communities. Connecticut College, in New London, sponsors an outstanding program in which students work and teach in the community. This is good for the town, good for the students, and very good for the college when it comes time for the special or annual appeal. It also helps attract the best students.

Corporate sponsorships are an important part of the fundraising efforts of the visionary trustee. In the case of the Shubert Performing Arts Center, sponsorships have been built around the charitable interests of the corporate sponsors so that the performances sponsored might be used as benefits for those charities of special interest to the corporate participant, in effect benefiting two organizations at once and leveraging the sponsor's investment. In one instance, an important corporate sponsor contributed to a performance at the Shubert to benefit a hospice organization and made a $50,000 gift to the Shubert in the bargain. Furthermore, making the theater available to other charities, such as hospitals, hospices, and social services organizations, for benefits of their own is a major line of business for the Shubert Performing Arts Center. As a result of these efforts and other programs involving visionary trusteeship, in less than eight years the Shubert has become an essential element of the cultural and philanthropic life of New Haven, which has produced major benefits for the Shubert's fundraising purposes.

Furthermore, as the arts are an essential ingredient in the ability of an urban environment to attract investment and the formation of capital, which is so vital to the economic development of any city, other nonprofits should strive to make a similar case to their donors, and to capitalize on opportunities to exploit it. In New Haven, the Shubert Performing Arts Center, in cooperation with the Arts Council of Greater New Haven and the University of New Haven, is conducting a sophisticated study to determine just how important the arts are to New Haven from an economic point of view. The Shubert will use the results to educate the entire community, including business and legislative leaders, about the economic value of the arts to the community and the crucial and pressing need for support.

If an organization can expand its influence and become helpful in a variety of ways, it will be all the harder to do without the organization. And if a community cannot do without it, the community will give money to support it.

Conclusion

The task confronting today's trustees, especially those with vision, is the selection of important strategies to persuade the appropriate constituencies to offer support. To accomplish this task, the trustee must have the vision to see the finished product and its potential benefit to the organization as well as to the donor. The visionary trustee is always thinking about how the organization can fulfill its public charge, whether by improving the quality of service or the ease of access, or by creating linkages that can expand the effect of the organization within its community. The visionary trustee thinks of ways to make the organization and its services relevant to its community so that it will be supported. The trustee charged with soliciting support must understand that the more hooks there are in the water, the more the program is likely to attract game fish. Vision, after all, is the art of keeping one's eyes open. Trusteeship is the art of acting on what one sees.

CHEEVER TYLER *is a lawyer in New Haven, Connecticut, where he currently serves as president of the Shubert Performing Arts Center and as chair of the board of the University of New Haven. He has been chair of the Distribution Committee of the New Haven Foundation, president and campaign chair of the United Way of Greater New Haven, and chair of the board of the Greater New Haven Chamber of Commerce, among other posts.*

Although nonprofit board members are often reluctant to get involved in fundraising, their roles and responsibilities are of serious consequence to nonprofit organizations. Board members can be motivated and trained to be of maximum benefit in resource development, and at the same time they can experience great satisfaction in their involvement.

3

The road least traveled: Board roles in fundraising

Lilya Wagner

JOHN D. ROCKEFELLER (1933) said, "Never think you need to apologize for asking someone to give to a worthy object." In truth, however, apologetic behavior about fundraising has been exhibited by many individuals important to the success of the nonprofit world. As consultant Thomas Broce (1986, p. 5) observed, "In the list of man's God-given characteristics the skill and the desire to ask people to give money to causes may not rank high." Sometimes, in fact, apologies border on downright avoidance of the issue and practice of fundraising.

 In the United States, where the methodology of philanthropic support is unique among all nations of the world, nonprofit board members sometimes say, "I'll do anything but raise money." Although board members are responsible for the financial viability of their organizations, some neither give money nor help get it.

NEW DIRECTIONS FOR PHILANTHROPIC FUNDRAISING, NO. 4, SUMMER 1994 © JOSSEY-BASS PUBLISHERS

Fundraising becomes the road least traveled by a significant number of these individuals. William H. Allen (1912, p. 177), who studied the seeking and giving of philanthropic support, recognized the seriousness of this situation: " 'Rubber stamping' trustees will never impress donors or public with the seriousness of benevolent work." He even called such behavior obstructive vagrancy.

However, volunteer board members are the most significant and powerful means for acquiring funds. If they gain a vision of possible human achievement for nonprofit causes, they may become motivated toward significant involvement in and contribution to a cause. What they need is to recognize their responsibility and valuable role in securing the success of an organization.

To achieve this desired state, boards need an opportunity to learn. Fundraising practitioners must communicate, educate, and relate to board members' attitudes and potential. Avoidance and apologetic attitudes can be transformed into adoption of responsibility and even enjoyment in presenting the organization's case to prospective donors. Three elements are necessary for achieving a fundraising board. First, members need to understand the significance of their roles and how these contribute to productive nonprofits. Second, board members and staff personnel must acknowledge and deal with attitudes that hinder positive involvement. Third, staff personnel, with the cooperation and blessing of the chief executive officer (CEO) and board chair, must communicate information—values, principles, practices—that leads to the adoption of appropriate board involvement.

Value of board participation in philanthropic fundraising

Experienced and knowledgeable development professionals verify the well-accepted fact that effective boards promote the causes of their organizations by securing the resources that support programs and services. Fortunately, a significant number of nonprofit board members in the United States also concur. They realize a sense of ownership and practice their role in fostering their organizations' success. They have moved beyond a rubber-stamping function. In doing so, they recognize their importance as volunteers in the non-profit world.

Brian O'Connell (1985, p. 120), while president of INDEPEN-DENT SECTOR, stated that "the fundraising commitment must begin with the board and must be high on the agenda of a significant number of the trustees. Not only must it be of high priority, it must also be high in status and recognition within the organization." Other highly respected professionals concur with this viewpoint. Henry A. Rosso, founder of The Fund Raising School, wrote that "willing involvement by board members in fundraising has been the hallmark of successful programs of past decades" (Rosso and Associates, 1991, p. 134). Maurice Gurin (1982, p. 65), an independent consultant now deceased, asserted that boards should recognize that they are central to the success of all fundraising, and that their strength in this effort determines the organization's fundraising effectiveness.

Fisher Howe, representative of Lavender/Howe and Associates, a management and fundraising consulting firm, is a respected authority on board development. Howe (1988, p. 1) identified five key principles of fundraising, the first of which is that "the board alone is ultimately responsible for attracting funding resources to ensure the financial viability of the organization and its programs." The board, according to Howe, must see to it that the organization has sufficient fiscal resources. Therefore, it must be involved in securing the necessary funds with the assistance of its peer members and supporting staff.

In discussing the eight fundamental responsibilities of a non-profit board, Andrew Swanson (1986a), an independent consultant, listed the raising and managing of the organization's funds. While recognizing that the board alone does not carry out all fundraising activities, he emphasized that the board must ensure that there is enough money to carry out the mission of the organization. The same has been said by Arthur C. Frantzreb, an independent consultant, who noted that the greatest single matter of concern for boards is financing the ongoing operation of an institution, therefore implying the board's responsibility for securing operating funds (Frantzreb, 1974).

Karl Mathiasen III (1990), founding director of the Management Assistance Group in Washington, D.C., identified three stages in a board's life cycle. First is the organizing board, followed by the volunteer governing board. The final stage is the institutional and fundraising board, which he calls a mature board. Mathiasen stated that a mature board accepts fundraising as a major and perhaps principal board activity. It pays attention to larger institutional concerns, primary of which is funding.

Generally, volunteer board members should be selected or invited on the basis of their affluence, influence, and commitment to the cause. Some trustees may join a board because of special constituency representation or expertise, but boards consisting of this type of members will not perform fundraising miracles. O'Connell (1985, p. 29) stated it this way: "I think it is fair to ask all board members, within their means and spheres of contacts, to contribute as much as they can and to help raise money. Asking for this help should be the responsibility of other volunteers and not the staff, and no board member should feel above these obligations." The staff, according to O'Connell, exists to help volunteers carry out the work of the organization, which includes fundraising.

Kenneth Dayton (1987, p. 9), former chair and CEO of the Dayton Hudson Corporation and current president of Oakleaf Foundation, recognized the importance of his role as one of O'Connell's INDEPENDENT SECTOR board members: "I look to him [O'-Connell] as our leader, our inspiration, our coordinator, our expediter, our doer. . . . But because we are a voluntary organization, I recognize that he can never do it alone or even do it with an excellent staff. . . . To be effective in his job, Brian needs hundreds, thousands, perhaps millions of volunteers to carry out the work of Independent Sector." Therefore, Dayton said, a trustee is both a governor and a volunteer.

A board member should contribute his or her resources to the organization because other donors look to the board for guidance. James Gregory Lord (1987, p. 52), an independent fundraising consultant, stated that "people will always ask, and with good reason: 'What did the board do?'" Lord went on to say that "the volunteer who solicits others without the benefit of a strong personal example is like the shoemaker who goes without shoes" (p. 53).

Nonprofit organizations exist because of donations from loyal constituents. Contributed funds sustain worthwhile programs. Boards have not only the responsibility but also the power and potential to acquire funds. The road least traveled does not have to be a board attitude. "I'll do anything but raise money" does not have to be in the board's vocabulary.

Attitudes of board members regarding fundraising

Kathleen Fletcher (1987), an independent California consultant, studied ten boards located near San Francisco. Board members were asked about their attitudes toward and participation in fundraising. Seventy-one members responded, and half said that they found fundraising to be distasteful, at least to some degree. On a brighter note, however, 75 percent indicated that they would ask for money if they *had* to, while 10 percent said that they would refuse.

When asked if board members should be actively involved in fundraising, 70 percent replied in the affirmative. However, only 25 percent had ever done personal solicitation. Most of those who participated in any fundraising effort had done so through a special event.

Board members surveyed in this study were not generous givers. Approximately 10 percent had not given personally to their organizations in the previous year, 60 percent had given over $50, and only 22 percent had donated more than $250. Regrettably, research studies like the one conducted by Fletcher (1987) are rare, but they should be replicated.

Board members often say, "I'll do anything but fundraising," for several reasons. Some find it generally distasteful. Some see it as begging. Others are reluctant to ask friends for funds, believing that they are taking advantage of friendships. Some fear rejection, and still others truly believe that they are not good at it. At times, board members are simply unsure how to proceed, and at other times they are genuinely fearful.

Robert J. Berendt and J. Richard Taft wrote a book for administrators in which they discussed how a CEO should evaluate an organizational fundraising program. They pointed out that "few board members ever join an institution because they enjoy fundraising and development. Indeed, among board members throughout the country, development and fundraising would, were a poll taken, probably rank as the most disliked responsibility in institutional stewardship" (1984, p. 28).

When motivations to serve on boards are enumerated, rarely if ever does the list include "desire to do fundraising." Some of these motivations are decidedly self-serving. Others, however, relate favorably to seeking and giving funds while allowing board members to realize their aspirations. A sample list was compiled by Donn F. Vickers (1990, p. 31), a consultant in organizational planning and staff development: political aspirations, business contacts, learning and self-improvement, commitment to a cause, status, affiliation need, utilization of talent, public visibility, development of a hobby or interest, exercising creative energy, and other.

There are, inevitably, individuals on any board who see no reason for serving beyond their own self-interest. Their excuses for not raising funds can be similar to those of board members who are more altruistic, but they cannot be moved or motivated to take action. John W. Gardner (1992, p. 1), founder of Common Cause and cofounder and first president of INDEPENDENT SECTOR, provided the following analysis: "There may be free riders on any board—people who do not fulfill their board duties responsibly. . . . Picking an arbitrary figure, I would say when the free riders constitute more than 25 percent of the total, look out!" It is important to distinguish between those board members who truly have legitimate fears and excuses and those who are the proverbial free riders. The former have positive potential, and their comments should be taken seriously. The latter are best left alone because, as more than one professional or active board member has said, "I would rather not have them do it at all than do it poorly." Some individuals of course, cannot ask for money, owing either to psychological hangups or physical handicaps. However, approximately 70 to 75 percent of board members could, and would be willing to, engage in their appropriate fundraising roles were the appropriate communication and education efforts implemented.

Howe (1991, p. 30) listed four ways in which boards often go wrong: "They fail to understand philanthropic giving and asking—to recognize that people want to give, that asking for support for a favorite organization is not preying on friends. They refuse to accept fundraising as their responsibility, one that cannot be passed off to someone else. They do not see the many things they can do to help in fundraising without ever directly asking for a contribution. And they are slow to realize that board members are motivated not by a general appeal, but rather by being asked personally to do specific tasks."

Board members become effective fundraisers when they understand the psychological principles of giving and receiving. Their role is critical in promoting the success of the giver-receiver relationship.

Fundraising practitioners' perceptions of board attitudes

Development professionals report, with alarming frequency, that boards have said, "We hired you to do the fundraising. You do it." Who is to do the fundraising? Swanson (1986b, p. 17) said that "too often, boards find it convenient to pass this responsibility over to staff, who, after all, are the experts and therefore (the rationalization goes) are best equipped to 'sell' the organization and its needs to potential donors. This, of course, is usually a fallacy." The most successful fundraising, Swanson went on to say, is carried out by peers in the community.

However, fundraising practitioners are not, by any means, absolved of responsibility for successful fundraising. Although board apathy and antagonism may exist, the situation is often exacerbated by poor relations, misunderstandings, and lack of communication between the board and professionals. For example, in a study reported in *Nonprofit Board Report* ("Most Nonprofits Don't Enforce Policy . . . ," 1992), two thousand nonprofit executives were asked, "Do you require board members to fundraise for your organization?" Only 39 percent said yes, while 58 percent responded no and 3 percent gave no answer. The question "Do you require board members to make a donation to your organization?" was asked of three thousand nonprofit executives. Of these, 27 percent said yes and 65 percent responded no; 8 percent did not respond.

There are several reasons why board members may not be as actively involved in fundraising as development officers desire. Professionals may forget that board members have to be *asked* to ask for money. A team approach, with communication and cooperation between staff and board, may not be a priority. Teamwork, the balance between board and staff functions, may not exist. The board may not realize and understand the staff's view of fundraising and its importance to the organization. Staff members, for whom cultivation, solicitation, and refusals are facts of life, may not comprehend the board members' true fear of solicitation and rejection. Fundraising may not be a board priority. Staff may not have given enough direction and encouragement to board members. Board members may not have experienced a successful encounter in securing funds, or even had previous experience. Also, staff may find board members unapproachable, perhaps due to their own perceptions of hierarchical structure within the organization or of physical and psychological distance between the board and staff. The development professional's perception of board attitudes is sometimes valid and realistic. At other times, perceptions obscure reality. The problem may lie in that fact that neither side understands or communicates with the other. Staff members must discern what stands between board members and fundraising success. Much can happen to benefit the organization if the professional accepts management responsibility for the fundraising process and communicates appropriately with the board.

A realistic approach to board participation in fundraising

Board members should be educated about philanthropy, its value to their organizations, and their critical roles and responsibilities. Although this instruction frequently is a staff responsibility, such efforts should be managed with the knowledge and cooperation of the board chair and CEO.

Education implies communication. However, barriers to communication exist in many board-staff relationships. Some of these are divergence of participants' backgrounds, differences in interest about the message, lack of mutual respect, lack of skill of the communicator, listener, or both, and lack of background information (Wilcox, Ault, and Agee, 1989). Each of these barriers can be applied to board-staff communication. For example, difference in interest about the message is certainly a serious consideration. Development staff, whose livelihood depends on successful fundraising, may have a different interest in the function from that of board members, who sometimes believe it is a staff function at best. Lack of mutual respect can also be a barrier. Development officers may not have earned, or even sought, the respect of board members and may be intimidated by them. In turn, development officers may have little esteem for board members, whom they view as arrogant but relatively ignorant about philanthropic fundraising. Development staff may also feel that board members demean the hired employee as a person of lower stature, and thus the staff may react with hostility or, at least, mistrust.

Communication regulators that restrict the absorption of new information further inhibit the board-staff relationship. When coupled with the barriers to communication, the situation is aggravated. George Gallup (Wilcox, Ault, and Agee, 1989, pp. 201–202) compiled seven regulators that hinder communication of new information and ideas (and much information about fundraising *is* new to board members): complexity of idea, difference from accustomed patterns, competition with prevailing ideas, necessity for demonstration and proof, strength of vested interests, failure to meet a felt need, and frequency of reminders. Again, each of these may inhibit board-staff communication regarding fundraising. Certainly, fundraising is a complex process and suffers from competition with other board responsibilities. Sometimes board members simply do not have a strong commitment to the organization's mission and programs. And most board members ask for proof of need before they commit themselves and their resources.

The difficulties enumerated above—the barriers and regulators that inhibit communication—must be surmounted before a team approach to fundraising can become a reality. Much of this can be accomplished through the five-stage adoption process presented by Wilcox, Ault, and Agee (1989): (1) *awareness:* a person becomes aware of an idea through communication; (2) *interest:* a person seeks more information about the idea; (3) *evaluation:* a person evaluates the idea on how it meets specific needs and wants; feedback from friends and colleagues is part of this step; (4) *trial:* a person tries the idea on an experimental basis; and (5) *adoption:* a person uses the idea on a regular basis and integrates it into his or her belief system. Each of these steps can be utilized in orienting, educating, and motivating board members to become active in fundraising.

Awareness

An understanding of the organization's mission and cause is critical in creating awareness of the board's roles and responsibilities in fundraising because the mission statement is a guide for the organization's activities. Peter F. Drucker (1992, p. 1), a highly respected management expert, stated that since nonprofits lack the bottom line of businesses, "they must therefore have a clear mission that translates into operational goals and that provides guides for effective action." Board members must see that devoting energy to the cause is worth the effort, and that they can accomplish this through an examination and reevaluation of the organization's mission.

Robert L. Thompson, chairman and CEO of Ketchum, Inc., stated that sometimes board members are uncomfortable in asking for money because "they've developed the erroneous idea that they're asking potential donors to respond to them rather than to the institution" (Ryan, 1989, p. 40). Board members need to see that they represent a cause larger than themselves. They must be assisted in developing ownership, pride, and enthusiasm for the institution. The key to this awareness step is focusing on mission and cause.

Fundraising staff can motivate the board by focusing on results, benefits, and success, rather than on problems (which should be acknowledged but not dwelt on). Board expectations of staff should be clarified, and, conversely, board members should clearly be told that their future involvement will not be more than they want to or are able to accomplish. A professional relationship between staff and board should be cultivated in the same manner as major-donor relations. When one or two members become advocates of the fundraising program, they in turn can influence their board peers and orient them toward positive attitudes and action.

As part of the awareness step, the board should be reminded (or informed) of truisms, such as those expressed by Howe (1988): People give money because they want to; people do not give unless they are asked; people give money to success, not distress.

Interest

Board members should be kept informed by the development professional regarding program details; in turn, members can serve as public relations representatives and speak on behalf of the organization. Such involvement will enhance the interest step in the adoption process.

Because board members have credibility and clout, they can aid a fundraising program by identifying, cultivating, and listening to prospects. They can also influence individual constituents or groups. They should share the results of their activity with the rest of the board and serve as examples of the value of board fundraising.

Board members need to feel useful. Some come with much enthusiasm, only to be ignored, perhaps unintentionally, by their peers, development professionals, or the CEO. Loss of interest and boredom due to lack of planning or underutilization of willing individuals can cause some members to drop out of the adoption process.

A board member may feel keenly about a two-sided issue—fear of soliciting and guilt for not soliciting. A practitioner can inform the reluctant member that fundraising is 90 percent preparation and 10 percent solicitation and that many roles, not just solicitation, are valuable in the fundraising process. These include qualifying prospects, participating in a direct-mail effort, and representing the organization to various constituent groups.

Evaluation

A board member can evaluate how he or she relates to the interest that has been developed at this point by positive interaction with peers or staff in activities that lead to personal solicitation. Specific assignments lessen anxiety and avoid confusion of roles and responsibilities. Positive and appropriate pairing of members with peers or staff is also vital. Fundraising information should continue to be shared regularly. Direct results of efforts and appropriate recognition are critical. If the board member experiences success through participatory planning, the evaluation process will lead to further involvement, or the trial step in the adoption process.

Trial

While converting interest into action, board members can serve their organization's fundraising efforts in a number of ways. At best, their experiences will lead to personal adoption of fundraising principles and practices, and at least they will be involved according to their individual strengths. Whatever the case, they will be experimenting with their own abilities and interests while assisting the organization with fundraising. Board members can recruit other volunteers, become increasingly involved in planning, share their enthusiasm and success stories with the entire board, and serve as ambassadors to selected constituent groups.

Members generally maintain their enthusiasm and confidence if appropriate rehearsal takes place. Trials should be translated into action as soon as possible.

Adoption

Once the adoption stage has been reached, the emphasis should be on profitable, feasible, valuable planned activity. Drucker (1992, p. 2) stated that "if they [board] have no legitimate function and no real job to do, they will do mischief; they will 'meddle.'" When interest has been developed, board members have personally evaluated the program as well as their own personal involvement levels. They have also experimented to the point of becoming active. Now a distinct focus for board activity must be maintained. "Boards should meddle," as Drucker (1992, p. 3) observed. "To begin with, there is no way to stop them, and if you can't lick them, you had better join them! . . . They had therefore better be organized so as to meddle constructively."

Constructive ways in which boards can remain involved include leadership roles on fundraising teams, advocacy of the institution, and recruitment of volunteers. The focus should continue to be on teamwork between board and staff and on maintenance of the critical balance between their respective roles. When the desired stage has been reached—probably not with the entire board but with a significant number of members—the focus should be on sustainability of successful fundraising programs.

Conclusion

The five-stage adoption process provides structure, coherence, and utility for much of what is known to succeed in motivating board members to engage in fundraising for their organizations. Within the framework of this process, the reflective fundraising practitioner can adapt and apply those principles and practices that will bring the greatest success to each individual set of people and circumstances. The committed board member can take on the primary responsibility of fundraising for the organization. This task is best facilitated by wise interaction and effective communication between board and staff, and by a clear understanding of each party's perceptions and apprehensions. While 100 percent cooperation is not feasible in most cases, teamwork can lead to success for boards, development professionals, and, ultimately, the organization. The road least traveled can be transformed into the road most traveled— fundraising involvement by nonprofit boards.

References

Allen, W. H. *Modern Philanthropy: A Study of Efficient Appealing and Giving.* New York: Dodd, Mead, 1912.

Berendt, R. J., and Taft, J. R. *How to Rate Your Development Office.* Washington, D.C.: Taft Corporation, 1984.

Broce, T. E. *Fund Raising.* Norman: University of Oklahoma Press, 1986.

Dayton, K. N. *Governance Is Governance.* Washington, D.C.: INDEPENDENT SECTOR, 1987.

Drucker, P. F. "Nonprofit Governance: Lessons for Success." Paper presented at the video teleconference A Crucial Partnership—Defining the Roles of Boards and Executives, Drucker Foundation Seminar, Apr. 1992.

Fletcher, K. B. "Increase Your Board's Fundraising: Suggestions from a Recent Study." *Nonprofit World*, 1987, *5* (3), 30–31.

Frantzreb, A. C. "Board Responsibility for Procurement of Resources." Paper presented for the Association of Governing Boards, Oct. 1974.

Gardner, J. W. "Board and Management." Paper presented at the video teleconference A Crucial Partnership—Defining the Roles of Boards and Executives, Drucker Foundation Seminar, Apr. 1992.

Gurin, M. *What Volunteers Should Know for Successful Fund Raising.* New York: Stein and Day, 1982.

Howe, F. *Fund Raising and the Nonprofit Board Member.* Washington, D.C.: National Center for Nonprofit Boards, 1988.

Howe, F. "Nonprofit Boards and Fund-Raising: Where They Are Likely to Go Wrong." *National Society of Fund Raising Executives Journal*, 1991, *16* (1), 28–30.

Lord, J. G. *The Raising of Money.* Cleveland: Third Sector Press, 1987.

Mathiasen, K., III. *Board Passages: Three Key Stages in a Nonprofit Board's Life Cycle.* Washington, D.C.: National Center for Nonprofit Boards, 1990.

"Most Nonprofits Don't Enforce Policy on Board Giving and Fundraising, Survey Shows." *Nonprofit Board Report,* Sept. 1992, pp. 1–2.

O'Connell, B. *The Board Member's Book: Making a Difference in Voluntary Organizations.* New York: Foundation Center, 1985.

Rockefeller, J. D. "The Technique of Soliciting." Address presented to the Citizens Family Welfare Committee, New York City, 1933.

Rosso, H. A., and Associates. *Achieving Excellence in Fund Raising: A Comprehensive Guide to Principles, Strategies, and Methods.* San Francisco: Jossey-Bass, 1991.

Ryan, E. "Advice to the Fundlorn." *CASE Currents,* 1989, *15* (10), 40–44.

Swanson, A. "The Role of the Board." *Nonprofit World,* 1986a, *4* (2), 15.

Swanson, A. "Who's in Charge Here?" *Nonprofit World,* 1986b, *4* (4), 17–19.

Vickers, D. F. *Partners in Leadership.* Columbus, Ohio: Leadership for the '90s, 1990.

Wilcox, D. L., Ault, P. H., and Agee, W. K. *Public Relations: Strategies and Tactics.* New York: HarperCollins, 1989.

LILYA WAGNER *is director of development at the National Association for Community Leadership, based in Indianapolis. She is former associate director of The Fund Raising School at the Indiana University Center on Philanthropy.*

This chapter explores the chief executive's role in the development of a successful board of trustees and presents a case study of how one agency makes it work.

4

Successful trusteeship: An executive director's viewpoint

David La Piana

FOR THE PAST TWELVE YEARS I have been executive director of East Bay Agency for Children (EBAC), a community-based nonprofit mental health agency serving children from birth to twelve years of age and their families in Alameda County, California. Eight years ago the agency served twenty children with one program, on a budget of $200,000. Today it serves over fifty-four hundred children in nine programs, many of them innovative prevention models, with a budget of $2.5 million from a complex web of public and private sources.

The EBAC Board of Trustees has twenty-four members and, in my (admittedly biased) opinion, is the most successful, functional voluntary agency board I have ever encountered. I believe there are several reasons for our board's success and that these reasons may have implications for other organizations.

Successful board of trustees

The obvious prerequisites for a successful board of trustees include an aggregate of intelligence, integrity, generosity, commitment, and

NEW DIRECTIONS FOR PHILANTHROPIC FUNDRAISING, NO. 4, SUMMER 1994 © JOSSEY-BASS PUBLISHERS

courage and the ability to sublimate personal needs to the greater good of the organization. The presence of these personal characteristics among trustees makes for a smoothly functioning group dynamic and the potential to achieve great things. But these attributes alone do not ensure success.

I have worked as line staff, middle manager, executive director, volunteer, trustee, or management consultant with more than three dozen nonprofit organizations. Most of the trustees I have met through these associations have, to one degree or another, displayed the positive characteristics enumerated above. Yet the vast majority of these agencies have failed to employ their trustees to either the organization's, or the trustees', maximum advantage.

Indeed, in my role as a nonprofit organization management consultant, I sometimes work with groups that are failing financially, programmatically, or organizationally, despite the goodwill and commitment of their boards of trustees. Often, I find trustees in such situations to be frustrated by a lack of timely, accurate information and stymied, intentionally or otherwise, by one another or by the agency executive. Moreover, they may fail to grasp conceptually the core of the challenges they face.

In these consulting roles I am repeatedly impressed by the disempowering effect of trusteeship on even the most successful business or civic leaders. For example, during a difficult and confounding discussion among the board of trustees of a voluntary agency floundering on the brink of insolvency, a fifty-year-old trustee, who owns a popular restaurant, meekly stated his confusion about whether it was the board or the chief executive who had authority to approve the organization's annual budget. Without information, and absent a definition of the trustee role in governance, confusion and acquiescence undercut the normal assertiveness of many trustees.

Compounding and intensifying this disempowering effect is the trustee who is unable to sustain a consistent level of involvement in the organization due to time constraints and competing priorities. Without regular participation, all but the most assertive trustees will be reluctant to ask probing questions; most will accept a certain level of confusion as the natural consequence of their poor attendance.

Admittedly, boards engaging a management consultant may constitute a sample skewed toward those in trouble, but I have observed these same dynamics and weaknesses in a wide variety of agencies that do not perceive themselves to be in crisis. I am confident that these descriptions are not unfamiliar to anyone who has served as a trustee of a voluntary agency.

Barriers to effective trusteeship

The reasons that so many organizations have not successfully activated their trustees on their behalf are varied. There are, however, certain common themes.

Differentiating governance and management

At one extreme is the organization that treats its executive director as a "gofer," with the board or individual trustees attempting to manage the agency. At the other end of the spectrum the executive is deferred to as a leader of almost messianic authority. Anything he or she says is believed, even when the financial statements, auditors, staff, consultants, or donors cry otherwise.

Difficulties such as these arise from a poor definition of the difference between management and governance, leading to the board's failure to govern, often with the complicity of the executive. The failure to distinguish between governance and management often results less from foggy organizational thinking than from group dynamics and the power struggles that individuals and groups carry on, often under a well-maintained cover of cooperation.

I have personally experienced such a struggle as a trustee. The agency executive in this example was competent and unfailingly polite, open, and thoughtful in his interactions with trustees. However, he could never quite find time to provide the information we requested. In fact, he presented himself as so harried and long-suffering that we began to feel guilty about troubling him with difficult questions—or with any questions at all for that matter.

The result was trustee withdrawal from governance, and an executive left in virtual control of the agency with little oversight. Next, some of our most capable volunteers began missing meetings and eventually resigned from the board.

Board's view of itself

Another common theme among less successful organizations is a board of trustees that tacitly sets a priori limits around its abilities, seeing itself as an observer rather than an actor in the drama of the organization's life. Volunteers may justify taking a backseat because an energetic, capable executive has the situation well in hand. Nonetheless, a reactive board of trustees almost ensures that the organization will fail to maximize its potential.

The terms *success* and *failure* are used here to refer to the daily grind of organizational life that reveals itself in small advances and retreats. I define success, not in terribly original terms, as sustainable, perceptible movement furthering the organization's mission. In my view, failure is anything short of this. In the quest for survival, so prominent in the minds of many executives and trustees, holding one's own is the acceptance of a failure to advance the mission.

Agency executives are not paid to hold their own. Trustees do not hope to simply maintain an even keel in the face of the massive challenges we are trying to address, in every field of voluntary agency endeavor. The public expects us to achieve results, and we should expect as much from ourselves: to improve children's lives; to house the homeless; to entertain, uplift, and instruct the public through the arts; to educate the young and the old; to heal the sick. These are results we must achieve, not merely principles to espouse, if we are to consider ourselves truly successful.

Role of planning

A third common theme among voluntary agencies that fail to actualize their potential is a misuse or misunderstanding of the role and power of planning. Organizations may stumble from one crisis to another, never tasting success, along the way blunting the appetite of desperate trustees for anything but stability. Such groups, it is easy to imagine, often produce reactive, conservative boards of trustees. Planning requires a certain level of confidence in the future, which may not be reasonable to expect of an agency in chronic crisis.

On the other hand, a great many organizations plan in a superficial manner. They argue passionately over the mission statement, they believe their own rhetoric about the strengths and weaknesses of the organization, and they devise ambitious goals that they would truly like to accomplish. Then they write up the plan, or their consultant does, and they are finished; the planning process over and done with.

In this scenario, which I have seen repeated numerous times, the plan is submitted to funders in grant request packages, taking advantage of its "artifactual value," and may be also dusted off occasionally to show to a prospective trustee. But, in fact, the plan has about as much bearing on the organization's future as last year's newsletter.

Finally, very few organizations still put the faith of a Stalin in "the five-year plan," stifling creativity among trustees and staff alike. The plan becomes a road map to success, and if circumstances should alter the destination or new opportunities should arise that lead to a rewarding detour, they are ignored.

Board-management culture

These three themes—the effective differentiation of the management and governance functions; the ability and willingness of trustees to view the voluntary agency as vital, potent, and developing; and the appropriate role and use of planning—describe dynamics that arise, are developed, and, ultimately, are expressed through the board-management culture. This culture, for good or ill, furnishes tacit agreements on the roles of trustees and management and on the potential, vision, and power of the organization and its place in the community. Out of this culture as well comes an orientation toward planning and toward action.

Role of the executive

So far, I have taken potshots, from the safety of the podium, at a full range of my colleagues, some of whom have paid me good money to help them through their crises. But I am not going to present EBAC as an oasis of success, peopled by smiling workers and motivated, magnanimous trustees, and overseen by a benevolent, omniscient, and infallible executive.

The problems that I have identified in other organizations I have also, obviously, observed within EBAC. They come with the territory for each executive director. Similarly, the weaknesses of executive directors presented here are more likely to result from inherent difficulties of the role than from the defects of an individual's character. The struggle for excellence is constant.

Especially in smaller organizations, the demands on the executive's time and talents are enormous. He or she must be all things to all people, with skills in an impossibly broad range of areas: accounting and finance, fundraising, human resources, computers, facilities management, real estate development, planning, public and media relations, and the law, to name a few general areas. In addition to these skills, a knowledge of the specific areas of the organization's endeavor (education, religion, health) is essential.

In many voluntary agencies the executive must also be available to work, for example, in the child care center, classroom, clinic, or gallery. In light of the many competing roles of the executive, and the constant struggle to make ends meet, it is not difficult to understand how the fine points of organizational development, however critical, get lost in the shuffle.

In fact, this chapter provides me an opportunity to explore the reasons why, despite the endemic problems of voluntary agencies, EBAC has been so successful. We have been successful in advancing our mission to improve the lives of children, and successful in doing so through the activation of our board of trustees.

Some executives argue that an active board of trustees is not necessary for success. A competent staff can sidestep the board, this argument goes, keeping trustees at arm's length. I have heard this view espoused by competent people who are frustrated by their inability to make their board "click" and so have given up trying. They have come to the unfortunate position of viewing trustees as a necessary evil.

It is impossible, however, to achieve success, that is, sustainable, perceptible movement furthering the organization's mission, without the thorough involvement of the board of trustees. After all, who but the volunteer trustee is the disinterested party representing the public interest in our organizations? Whose mission is it, anyway? Staff, no matter how competent and dedicated, are hired hands. The community's best interests are safeguarded by the establishment and pursuit of a mission by the community's representatives, the volunteer trustees.

East Bay Agency for Children

EBAC's success has been achieved through the conscious development of a culture that supports active trusteeship. The term *organizational culture* implies an unconscious accumulation of habits and interactional modes that reveal and reinforce certain shared values. Increasingly, however, as we see the pervasive effects of organizational culture on everything from the bottom line and competitiveness to quality outcome and workplace satisfaction, conscious attempts to modify the culture are being initiated. This is precisely what we have attempted at EBAC over the past twelve years.

EBAC's twenty-four trustees are partners with management in exploring and deciding governance issues. By design, the board spends far more of its meeting time discussing the "higher plane" issues of vision, mission, and direction than it does poring through the nitty-gritty of the quarterly financial statements, whose consideration and analysis is largely carried out in committee. One trustee commented, "On the ballet board we spend two hours haggling over finances, and then give fifteen minutes to the artistic director to present his proposals for next season's shows. At EBAC we spend ten minutes on a succinct report from the finance committee and leave an hour to discuss the development of a new, badly needed service or some other staff 'brainstorm.'"

EBAC's board of trustees is focused on the larger issues, but it is also committed to specific results. Within the culture, trustees are viewed as indispensable actors who guard the organization's mission and take responsibility individually and corporately for its achievement.

For example, EBAC's first strategic plan was created in 1986. Through the planning process, we decided to open a new site thirty miles away, doubling the agency's size. Once the vision of a wider service area was accepted, trustee support for the endeavor was absolute.

A year later it became clear that ongoing growth required a new headquarters facility. The board of trustees responded by approving a capital campaign goal at a level that would have seemed unthinkable a year earlier. This was also a time when program growth was averaging 50 percent a year and the need for a second new facility in our newly expanded service area was also looming on the horizon.

We undertook the campaign without outside fundraising counsel. Each trustee made a sacrificial gift to the effort, setting the campaign's pace, and accounting for more than 25 percent of the total raised. The board's level of giving spurred individual trustees to become aggressive solicitors. Within a year we exceeded our campaign goal and, with staff matching the board's commitment and resourcefulness, completed construction in record time and on budget.

I mention both raising the money and completing the project in the same sentence to make an important point: the volunteer trustee role and the professional staff role forever reinforce each other for better or for worse. Staff support makes volunteer success possible, which in turn enables staff to succeed. Volunteer success also demands staff success to validate its own effort.

If the campaign had been successful but construction had bogged down and was finally completed well over budget, this staff failure would have invalidated the trustees' effort and set the stage for future board failure. Instead, a crisply executed building schedule reinforced the trustee effort and set the standard for future board planning and action.

Developing an effective board-management collaboration

What factors contribute to the development of a successful board-management culture and collaboration? In addition to mutual expectations of success and reciprocal reinforcement, trustees and management must develop and sustain mutual respect, trust, and positive regard.

Ongoing board training, development, and empowerment must be organized to promote a sense of shared ownership of the organization. Trustees are to be engaged in the struggle, not merely fed information. The analogy that comes to mind is the difference between experiencing a kiss and hearing one described: There is no comparison.

The executive director must make an absolute commitment to keep the board informed of all pertinent information and developments, not just of matters that reflect well on him or her, in a timely and efficient manner. This commitment says, "I give you information because you have as much of a stake as I do in the organization's success."

The executive must also be willing to present information and decision options in a truly open manner. Trustees sense when the executive does not want to hear their opinions. Have you ever sat in a board meeting trying to get answers from a likable, dedicated, overworked, underpaid executive who seemed unable to grasp your question? Or whose evasiveness made you feel like a cross-examining lawyer, framing your questions carefully to get the answers you needed?

This lack of frankness, intentional or careless, leads to volunteer distrust and disengagement. As a consultant, I have seen it lead to the loss of influential community supporters, to factionalization into pro- and anti-executive camps on the board, to hasty and poor decision making, and, ultimately, to major setbacks for the organization.

While trustees and management share responsibility for the organization's success, I lay responsibility for sustaining a culture that encourages board ownership of and involvement in the organization at the feet of the executive. He or she has the information, is involved with the issues full-time, and is in the leadership role. The executive sets the organizational agenda. The development and sustenance of an effective board of trustees is the executive's "Job 1."

If you accept this premise, it follows that the executive must take responsibility for his or her board's functioning and determine to push hard to improve it. For the trustee serving on an executive selection committee, my advice is to probe candidates carefully on their thinking and experience and the value they place in this area. Speak to trustees at organizations where the candidates were formerly employed. You will hear a ringing endorsement of an "involver."

The trustee of an organization experiencing some of the difficulties described here has a most difficult task. Ask questions, demand answers, force the organization to look at itself and where it is going. If the executive rises to the occasion, you have done a great service for everyone. If he or she becomes defensive or tries to sidetrack the process, you have the wrong person in the job. If the board threatens to break up into factions around this issue, get help from outside.

Encouraging active trusteeship

Let me get specific about the ways in which EBAC encourages active trusteeship. We have consciously cultivated the involvement of trustees through the following means:

1. Board meetings begin and end on time and are run with a crisp sense of purpose. No one feels that his or her time is being wasted. This may seem obvious, but think about the meetings you attend: Do they begin and end on time? If not, how does it make you feel? Are the meetings on track? Do they accomplish anything? After the meeting, do you receive feedback demonstrating that decisions made are being implemented? Again, if not, how do you feel about an agency that frustrates you and perhaps wastes your time?

2. EBAC promotes regular trustee contact with service-providing staff, not just managers, at retreats, special focus items at board meetings, and informal family picnics and parties. In this way EBAC provides trustees with access to different views of the organization, counters any tendency for volunteers to think management might be packaging the agency for trustee consumption, and motivates the board to support the valiant efforts of the frontline staff.

3. Information flow to trustees is timely and regular. Meeting notices, agendas, and minutes are mailed out at the same expected time each month. Trustee requests for information are answered promptly, usually the same day.

4. Policy decisions are framed in a manner helpful to trustees, who have limited time to delve into the minutiae of agency operations. Alternatives and consequences are spelled out, but room is left for trustees to draw their own conclusions or suggest other approaches.

5. Practical help from trustees is welcomed. Volunteers with legal, fundraising, and financial management expertise work with staff regularly or on special projects.

6. As in most organizations, managers provide staff support for board committees. However, the president and the executive director also attend virtually all committee meetings, emphasizing th~ seriousness of their work. At board meetings, trustees and managers give due credit to those who have performed outstanding services for EBAC.

7. Management "talks success" all the time to one another and to trustees. We expect success, we view setbacks as only temporary, and we constantly point to the mission as our beacon. The staff's enthusiasm is infectious.

8. The staff also regularly produces success, making EBAC trusteeship an opportunity to participate in a dynamic, "up" organization. This atmosphere is particularly motivating to volunteers, in combination with the compelling stories of so many of our clients. Society may be going to hell in a handbasket, but our program growth is averaging 20 percent annually during a recession, more in better times, and we are effectively helping more children each year.

9. The executive director is not a board officer or trustee. EBAC honors and upholds the trustee role as voluntary.

The result of all of the above is a board of trustees that to a large degree feels ownership of the organization, a connection to the individuals who work for it, and a sense of shared purpose. Ninety percent of trustees could tell a stranger what EBAC does, how long it has been doing it, what is in our budget, how many children we serve, and where we are going. An even greater number, according to a recent internal survey, would also tell anyone who asked that our work is one of the most important activities going on in our community.

The firestorm

The close identification of trustees with EBAC was brought home most poignantly in October 1991. EBAC is located in Oakland, just a stone's throw from the firestorm burn area. On the afternoon and evening of October 20, two of our staff and five trustees lost their homes and all of their possessions. More than a dozen former trustees and active supporters were also among the more than thirty-five hundred families burned out. Tragically, one former trustee was killed.

On Monday morning, October 21, with the fire still not totally contained, several staff assembled at our headquarters office, despite eye-irritating smoke and an understandable desire to be with their families during the crisis. Phone calls poured in all day from

trustees and donors. They wanted to know if EBAC was still safe-
ly standing, they wanted to tell us their status and leave phone numbers where they could be reached, and they wanted to know if their
friends and neighbors had called. Mostly, they wanted to make a familiar connection during a frightening time. Somehow, they knew
that their friends, too, would check in with EBAC in the crisis.

There was a high degree of confusion that Monday morning.
News reports were contradictory about both the status and extent
of the fire. Then my wife called: A house a block away from ours
was burning. I rushed home to evacuate my family. Fortunately, the
fire department arrived quickly and the fire, caused by burning de-
bris that flew two miles from the fire area, was quickly extinguished.

I returned to the office. Information was scanty, but the calls continued to come in. So we set up an impromptu clearinghouse, post-
ing the status of each of our callers, and reading the information
off to anyone who subsequently called in. By the end of the day we
got out a memo to trustees sharing all of the information we had
gathered.

We received a report of an entire block burned. Three trustees
who lived there lost everything. Then we received a report of an
adjacent block burned. Another trustee lived on this block. We reported his house lost. Somehow word got to him and he called in.
The fire had indeed burned his block, but miraculously his home
was spared by the two-thousand-degree conflagration.

When it was all over and I had time to think, I reflected on the
curiously strong connection that people must feel to EBAC to call
us just hours after losing their homes or while still under evacua-
tion order. They cared about EBAC, yes, and they knew we would
worry about them. But somehow they also assumed, correctly it
turned out, that other trustees would call in, and so EBAC was a
place to get information.

Since I am in the mental health field, I am entitled to look for
symbolism and motivation. Here it is. Not only do our trustees
have a strong, emotional connection to EBAC, but they also believe, even under very difficult circumstances, that they are able to

get information from us. They feel that somehow, if the world is falling apart, we will still be functioning. This is the truest portrait of our board-management culture.

Summary: *The executive's most significant effort*

To summarize, the successful employment of volunteer trustees rests on the development and maintenance of a culture that expects their contributions, rewards their efforts, and encourages their ownership. Many pressing claims on the executive's time compete with the efforts necessary to develop and sustain an active and involved board. Over time, however, this is the single most significant effort the executive can make to ensure organizational success.

DAVID LA PIANA, M.P.A., *is executive director of East Bay Agency for Children, a Northern California mental health agency. He is also a management consultant for nonprofit and public agencies and an adjunct faculty member at the Institute for Nonprofit Organization Management, University of San Francisco.*

A series of interviews with staff and trustees of not-for-profits with a record of successful fundraising offers a model for staff and trustee interaction in the fundraising process.

5

Trustees and staff: Building effective fundraising teams

Timothy L. Seiler, Eugene R. Tempel

OUR THEORY that staff play an indispensable role in fundraising, although they often underestimate their importance, led us to study the role of staff and the nature of their interaction with volunteers in the fundraising process. Inasmuch as volunteers occasionally feel that an increased staff role in fundraising can reduce their importance, we decide to investigate tensions that might exist when staff and volunteers interact. We posed the following questions: How do board members and staff view each other? What do board members expect of professional staff, and staff of board members?

We limited our investigation to organizations committed to successful use of volunteers in peer solicitation. The role of staff in this setting is to have the right volunteers solicit the right prospects for appropriate gifts. Staff, then, must interact successfully with volunteers, who usually are community leaders accustomed to managing and leading. How do staff provide leadership in this process? How do they lead the leaders? And what must volunteers do to be successful in a process in which they take their lead from staff?

NEW DIRECTIONS FOR PHILANTHROPIC FUNDRAISING, NO. 4, SUMMER 1994 © JOSSEY-BASS PUBLISHERS

What tensions exist in this role inversion in which leaders—the volunteers—find themselves following the direction of the staff?

To understand better the dynamics of volunteer-staff relationships in the fundraising process, we searched the literature on trustee involvement in fundraising and surveyed organizations that have successfully involved trustees in fundraising. We wanted to determine if these two sources of information could help us answer our questions and develop a model for successfully involving trustees in fundraising.

Our literature search provided no specific information about trustee-staff interaction in fundraising. Although much has been written about trustee responsibilities for nonprofit organizations, along with some work on trustee responsibilities in fundraising (see, especially, Ingram, 1988; O'Connell, 1987), our search disclosed no published material on the interaction between trustees and staff in carrying out successful fundraising. Writers on board involvement in fundraising call for greater trustee involvement, but they do not define how boards can become involved, nor do they discuss the role of staff in building this involvement. We did, however, find a number of related sources that provide contextual background for discussion of the issue.

With help from Pat Lewis, president of the National Society of Fund Raising Executives, and Charles Johnson, vice president for development of the Lilly Endowment, we compiled a list of organizations that successfully engage trustees in fundraising. We interviewed their trustees and senior development staff, using a series of questions designed to determine what expectations staff and volunteers have of each other in the fundraising process. These questions are listed in Appendixes A and B of this chapter. Our goal was to develop information about successful interaction between staff and trustees in fundraising, rather than to gain insights into the range of trustee engagement among different organizations. We were interested in building a model for successful trustee-staff interaction, not in developing a status report on trustee-staff interaction. Since we were aware of the tension inherent to having leaders follow and followers lead, and the potential tension in professional and volunteer relationships, we asked staff members to describe relationships between themselves and trustees in carrying out fundraising tasks.

Related perspectives

Our search of the literature disclosed no published sources to help us understand how to engage trustees successfully in fundraising and the role of staff in doing so. We discovered, however, a number of related sources that provided useful perspectives for our study of trustee-staff interaction.

Because the context for our study is organizations committed to the service of volunteers, especially trustees, in fundraising, a discussion of the significance of that role is relevant here. Henry A. Rosso addressed the topic directly (Rosso and Associates, 1991, pp. 133–134). He stated that after eighteen years of teaching some fifteen thousand students in The Fund Raising School, the most common problem reported by participants is trustee apathy and unwillingness to become involved in fundraising.

Rosso argued that a trustee, as a primary steward of an organization, "must be more than an overseer, a custodian, a casual adviser, a sometime participant, an absentee member, a misguided volunteer apt to confuse administration with governance, or a vociferous adversary maintaining steadfastly that gift making and gift seeking are definitely not the responsibility of a board member. A trustee must be willing to espouse the cause of the organization by assisting it in securing the resources that are necessary to support the programs that are required by the statement of mission" (Rosso and Associates, 1991, p. 134). With increasing competitiveness among nonprofits and with closer scrutiny of and greater accountability for contributed dollars, Rosso believes that trustees must be in the forefront of fundraising for "the programs and services they have reviewed, approved, and put in place as members of the governing board" (p. 134), and that if we lose trustees as active fundraisers, organizational fundraising will lose a great deal. The most powerful "ask" the organization can make is through a trustee who has made his or her own gift: "Gift making reflects a commitment. It states forthrightly, 'I believe. I can affirm the values of this program. And because I believe, I have made my own gift, and I am asking you to join with me in support of this most important work'" (p. 138).

In his writing on boards, Cyril O. Houle also has discussed the responsibility of fundraising. Of eleven major responsibilities of board members, the ninth is, "The board must accept responsibility for securing and managing adequate financial resources" (Houle, 1989, p. 93). While Houle believes that it is a dismal oversimplification to choose board members only because of their ability to give, raise, and manage money, these are "given prominence because the securing and handling of funds are both essential to operation and a matter about which board members are often able and well informed. They understand both the importance of continuing financial health and the procedures required to ensure it" (1989, p. 93).

Tensions in trustee-staff interaction during fundraising may result because trustees of nonprofit corporations often look to the corporate boards with which they are familiar for their role models. According to Houle (1989, p. 93), many for-profit corporations resemble nonprofit institutions, but a key difference between the boards of the two types of organizations is that corporate boards "tend to be validating committees, ratifying decisions made elsewhere." Board members are generally officers of the company, not representatives of the diversity of the community.

Because corporate boards consist largely of corporate executives, they tend to be mainly top-down in their approach to policy once it is ratified. Nonprofit boards tend to be top-down only in approving and forwarding policy, especially when that policy has involved consultation with outside or external constituents as it was developed.

But there is another important area of distinction between for-profit and nonprofit boards. Trustees of nonprofit organizations must be willing to take direction from staff in fulfilling their volunteer roles, especially in fundraising, while they reserve the right to set policy for the organization's staff to implement. Corporate board members would never expect to be asked by subordinates to carry out operational tasks for the organization.

Many experts on boards have tried to distinguish between board and staff as follows: Boards set policy, and staffs carry it out. Houle (1989, p. 15) seems to agree with Brian O'Connell (1987), president of INDEPENDENT SECTOR, that the distinction is not that simple: "Boards must perform a number of executive and judicial functions, such as selecting an executive, carrying on financial campaigns, authorizing large purchases, arbitrating serious conflicts, and performing volunteer services for the program." Houle and O'Connell seem to promote the concept that board members will at times carry out management tasks, including fundraising. This ultimately raises the question of the roles of staff in supervising trustees who become involved in carrying out management tasks as volunteers.

Board and staff must interact to make certain that board members operate on the basis of their belief in the organizational mission. Board members' advocacy for their organizations is the key component of the successful board-staff team. Trustees must be in the forefront of volunteer efforts for fundraising. Staff members must contribute to the team by modeling fundraising leadership through performance and example.

Although Houle and O'Connell view the involvement of trustees in fundraising as essential to success and provide insights into the potential tensions that can result, they do not discuss how to involve trustees in fundraising and how to build the effective trustee-staff teams that they recommend.

Paul J. Ilsley (1990, p. 77) discussed tensions inherent to relationships between paid staff and volunteers in nonprofit organizations. While his work is focused primarily on volunteers who are engaged in providing direct services to clients, his observations provide a context for examining trustee-staff relationships in the fundraising process. Ilsley argued that "volunteer organizations are becoming increasingly professional, as shown by an emphasis on standards of practice (including certification of volunteers, new rules for accountability, and stricter training regimens) as well as by the increased allocation of resources toward organizational maintenance" (p. 77).

Increasing professionalism is one of the potential threats to building effective trustee-staff teams. Ilsley (1990, p. 80) listed several events that are likely to occur as a volunteer organization becomes more professional. Among these are increases in the proportion of the organization's budget spent on managing volunteers through selective training, certification, specialization, and supervision and increases in the alienation of volunteers from paid staff and in the frequency of perceptions of volunteers, their clients, and the public that the organizational system is degrading. If trustees see themselves as being directed in formal, authoritative ways by paid fundraising staff who see themselves as professionals, the relationship might become less satisfactory for the trustees.

Ilsley (1990, p. 111) indicated that the best situations for volunteers are in organizations where managers trust them (rather than distrust or tolerate them). He noted that managers who trust volunteers speak about them with great enthusiasm and seem to operate their organizations in a more open, less formal style that enhances volunteer satisfaction.

In the context of delivery of services, Ilsley (1990, p. 122) discerned potential conflict: "The sphere of the paid staff is a powerful one. Its aim is to uphold the professional standards of an organization such as standards of education in schools, library science in libraries, nursing in hospitals. Conflict is likely to result whenever staff members see volunteers as a threat to their professionalism."

Viewpoints of successful executives and trustees

With little information available to help us understand the dynamics that enable trustees and staff to work together effectively in fundraising, we interviewed successful nonprofit executives, fund-raising executives, and trustees. Several of those with whom we spoke minimized potential tensions between trustees and staff, not-ing that diversification of boards has reduced socioeconomic gaps between trustees and staffs. Most acknowledged, however, that the threat of potential tensions is real and that they work deliberately to enable staff to provide leadership for trustees in fundraising.

Edward Ellis, executive director of the Presbyterian Hospital Foundation in Charlotte, North Carolina, addressed this issue very well. When asked if his staff members enjoy their working rela-tionships with trustees, he replied, "Enjoy it? Yes. Have anxiety about it? Yes. The anxiety is caused by the fact that trustees are pow-erful, rich, famous people about whom the staff members read in the newspaper. Staff members are honored just to be in the room with them. I try to coach my staff through this anxiety. I ask them to notice how much the trustees enjoy being with us. I ask them to see how much the trustees believe in the organization we represent. I ask them to notice how much the trustees count on us and how important we are to them."

Those interviewed suggested that staff members become effec-tive team members on the trustee-staff fundraising team as they gain experience and develop professionally. This suggests that the staff role on the team is based on acquired skills.

Both fundraising executives and trustees of organizations that successfully engage staff and trustees in fundraising have no diffi-culty enumerating or listing professional skills that staff members bring to relationships with trustees in the fundraising process. The first asset that both trustees and executives listed is expertise in the process itself. Executives believed that this is one of the critical el-ements in building relationships with trustees to help them succeed. Trustees cited fundraising expertise as the basis for their reliance on staff members. Trustees respected and appreciated the profes-sionalism among staff. Thus, staff members should be made aware of this factor and concentrate on building their levels of expertise. Several executives reported enhancement of these qualities through staff participation in conferences and courses.

Several individuals also stressed the importance of experience, both in depth and variety. Others stressed the importance of a record of success in fundraising as a qualifying skill that staff persons bring to the trustee-staff team. Claudia Looney, senior vice president of Saddleback Memorial Foundation and chair of the National Society of Fund Raising Executives Foundation, said that "their knowledge base and their successful track records empower our staff. They are also empowered through attending educational conferences and becoming certified or accredited fundraisers."

Confidence in professional staff also depends on concepts of ethics and on protection of the donors' interests. Albert Hally, who was a trustee and a chair of the Saddleback Memorial Foundation Board, cited this confidence as one of the critical elements in successful trustee-staff solicitations. Speaking of a staff person, he said, "He considers the donor's perspective. We [trustees] are always confident that the relationship we have with the prospect will be protected during the solicitation."

Another important skill cited by both trustees and executives is knowledge of volunteer management and sensitivity to trustees' needs. Both groups saw this as a professional level skill. Several individuals stressed the importance of knowing how to encourage, motivate, and "push trustees to action" without nagging, without being directive and authoritative, and of knowing when to back off and give trustees some space.

Both trustees and executives also cited as a staff member skill knowledge about the community, about the prospects, and about the information-gathering or research process. While organizational insiders might see this as a particular strength of trustees, the executives reported it as an important skill of their staffs and trustees saw it as a strength that staff members bring to the trustee-staff fundraising team.

Another asset that staff members bring to the trustee-staff fundraising team is firsthand knowledge of the organization's programs. While trustees did not list this as one of the skills that staff members bring to the team, most executives did. Several cited staff knowledge of the organizations' missions and programs as the basis for staff to educate trustees and provide leadership. Edward Ellis considered staff knowledge about the organization a priority in staff development: "We orient our staff so they are thoroughly familiar with the services provided by our hospital and the issues involved in health care delivery. This is very important. It provides a knowledge base which allows staff to educate trustees. This educational capability gives them a position of strength from which to deal with trustees. We involve our staff in department head meetings even though they are not department heads. They feel important and understood by their colleagues."

Other staff qualities cited by those interviewed include organizational skills, strategic thinking skills, enthusiasm, pride in the work they do, and support and detail management skills. Altogether, the skills that staff members bring to the trustee-staff team enable them to fill roles on the team with confidence.

When executives were asked how they empower staff to deal with trustees who come from a more influential socioeconomic background, they generally again referred to the skills that staff members bring to these relationships. Enhancing knowledge of the fundraising process and of the organization was cited as a primary way of empowering staff. Self-confidence was cited as a key.

Ellis also stressed the importance of developing leadership skills in young staff persons so that they can approach trustee relationships with confidence. He described the process of involving staff with trustees: "I was mentored into trustee work by someone who helped me. I try to mentor my own staff by including them when I meet with trustees. I try to demonstrate to them how one interacts with trustees. This provides backup for me and gets them involved. It also helps to legitimize relationships between my staff members and trustees." Charles Stephens, director of development and communication at the Indiana University Center on Philanthropy, made a similar point: "You cannot empower yourself. That must be done by the chief executive officer of the organization." He also described the ideal staff-trustee relationship as one of mutual respect. Claudia

Looney also cited open access to trustees as a key to making the relationship work. Her organization allows all staff members who need to involve trustees in fundraising direct access to them.

The staff members whom we interviewed described their relationships with trustees as one of mutual respect and trust. They also saw themselves as taking the lead in initiating fundraising. Staff generally viewed themselves as driving the fundraising process, with the trustees taking suggestions and receiving support in completing the fundraising tasks.

The common theme sounded by staff members is that successful relationships between staff and trustees must be based on partnership. Staff are often organizers who provide information to trustees and who gently remind them of their fundraising tasks. Board members occasionally require administrative and follow-up support and occasionally need a staff person to take control and move the process forward. Successful relationships are built on the ability of staff members to play whatever role is needed by individual board members. Ann Meier, director of trustee services for the American Symphony Orchestra League, summarized this idea: "Partnership must be one of mutual dependence—trustees must depend on staff to pay attention to things they don't have time for on a daily basis." Staff best provide leadership by asking important questions prior to board members' enlistment: Do they have time to dedicate to this organization? Do they have the energy to do the job?

While current literature on fundraising calls for greater board leadership, our interviews revealed that professional staff in successful fundraising organizations saw themselves in professional leadership positions. Further, they believed that board members expect such leadership from staff. Based on thirty-seven years of experience with boards, Herbert Jones, recently retired from his position as vice president for development at the Indianapolis Symphony Orchestra, is committed to staff members taking leadership roles in initiating and guiding trustees' actions in the fundraising process. Jones described the successful staff person as one who "subtly provides direction to the process. Staff must be persistent to keep trustees moving along." The word "subtly" may be the key here, given a response of Mary Gates, who was a regent at the University of Washington. When asked if she expected staff to take a leadership role and provide direction and guidance, she replied, "Leadership role? Yes, if this means applying professional expertise to the situation and speaking in an honest and candid way about the pros and cons of issues. Direction? No. Guidance? Absolutely."

Jones summed up the ideal staff-board relationship by listing factors essential to success, such as honesty, candor, initiative, and follow-through. Professional staff are "educators, informers, and enablers. We simply have to be empathetic. People of wealth, power, and influence need people in whom they can place their trust in helping them achieve their objectives. This is a great opportunity development officers have."

Based on the experiences of successful professional staff fundraisers, what factors are necessary in establishing a working relationship with trustees that leads to success in fundraising? The words we heard most often were "partner" and "partnership." Successful staff persons accept their responsibility to provide leadership and take initiative in fundraising; at the same time, they acknowledge that their full partner in the process is the board volunteers. There must be mutual trust and respect between staff and trustee.

H. Perrin Anderson, chairman of the board of trustees of Presbyterian Hospital in Charlotte, North Carolina, echoed this theme of mutual trust. He said that "the key to successful trustee-staff fundraising is mutual respect and understanding." He clarified this by adding that trustees must understand the professional skills that staff bring to the process, and staff members must respect the extensive demands made on trustees by their various professional and personal roles.

Martha Bracher, director of development for The Center for Contemporary Arts of Santa Fe, said, "There needs to be a mutual willingness to support each others' needs. Success is based on follow-through: You must do what you say you will do." Bracher treats her board members the same way she treats her staff, as individuals. She also regards her board members as bosses and provides them whatever they need to succeed in fundraising: "I work very closely with my board, and they know they are expected to be involved in the fundraising process for twelve months of the year. Each board member is expected to be part of a solicitation team and to give an individual gift. They are also expected to identify other prospective givers." Bracher described this interaction with board members in fundraising as "thrilling and rewarding. It is an absolutely enjoyable experience, forming friendships and gaining knowledge and experience from board members." She noted that trust is essential for this interaction and believed that her board members recognized her commitment and dedication to the task and thus trusted her and her judgment: "I see myself and my board members as equals. We may disagree, but we respect each other, and when working for our organizations we are equal partners."

Nancy Axelrod, executive director of the National Center for Nonprofit Boards, expressed the view that success in fundraising is built on a clear "strategy which is more than a series of noble intentions." Board members must understand their responsibility to raise funds, and the organization must be clear in its expectations of board members. She described her trustees as "helpful and supportive of fundraising initiatives from the staff. The directors expect staff to take the lead and give direction." She described her own role as "helping to enlist board members in the process." Overall, "the ideal relationship between staff and trustees is built on executives willing to devote time and energy to fundraising and able professionals to provide leadership and follow-up support to back the board members. Essential to success are belief in the mission of the organization and pride in its accomplishments." Axelrod reported that most of the fundraising in her organization is done by the staff and that the board "is capable of and willing to do more." In her approach, the staff's responsibility is to provide direction and to determine how best to use the time and expertise of individual trustees. Describing the relationship between herself and her board members as one of mutual respect, Axelrod said that staff earn this respect through "a willingness to make an investment in the fund-raising process. Success in fundraising is probably the best qualifi-cation" for staff to be able to assume a leadership role.

Kenneth Gladish, executive director of the Indianapolis Foun-dation, confirmed the importance of staff leadership and the need for partnership relations. On the former, he stated, "The board takes the initiative in strategizing and planning, and the staff take the initiative in reaching fundraising goals." He emphasized the im-portance of staff members being judicious in their leadership roles, involving board members as colleagues. Gladish described the ide-al arrangement as a "partnership in which we are all colleagues in the whole fundraising effort, from determining organizational needs to the solicitation of support to evaluating the process." He believes that even though the literature consistently calls for trustee leadership in fundraising, the norm is "almost always that chief pro-fessional officers are in leadership roles."

Polly Jontz is the president of Conner Prairie, a living-history museum north of Indianapolis where the year is always 1836. She works with a development committee of the board that governs Conner Prairie. Jontz believes that professional staff play an im-portant leadership role in involving trustees in fundraising. She not-ed that the skills she and her staff bring to the process are a knowledge of the donors' interests, experience in the fundraising process, and attention to detail. Suggesting that staff must "en-courage without nagging" trustees, Jontz described the ideal rela-tionship as one where staff and trustees can "be open, share information, and be discreet." Staff members need to remind trustees of deadlines and where they stand in making calls. Essen-tial to fundraising success is the staff's ability to be cheerleaders, to create trustees' enthusiasm. For Jontz, it is "a privilege to work with people who are successful, energetic, and achieving. It is reward-ing to work with people like this and is one of the most enjoyable things I do."

The ideal relationship of mutual respect and trust described by those we interviewed resembles the servant-leader concept of

Robert Greenleaf (1977). The servant-leader is one who aspires to serve first, then to lead. Through serving others by meeting their needs, a servant-leader assumes the role of leader. Greenleaf (1977, p. 15) described the servant-leader as an individual who is "better than most at pointing the direction. By clearly stating and restating the goal, the leader gives certainty and purpose to others who may have difficulty in achieving it for themselves."

It is the complementary abilities and skills of trustees and staff that nurture the trusting relationships that in turn lead to success in fundraising. The special contacts and the skill and grace of trustees make possible the successful solicitation of community leaders. The professional competence of staff enables them to skillfully move the solicitation process forward from start to finish. Acceptance of the interdependence of trustees and staff, and a willingness to step forward as leaders at one time and as servants at another, underlie the partnership necessary for success.

Staff members must work at making fundraising easy and comfortable for trustees. This means taking the initiative in leadership or providing follow-up detail work, or whatever else trustees require of staff. As Gladish reported, "These activities of staff are mutually reinforcing. Follow-up is not necessary without leadership; leadership is not possible without the fundraising context."

As staff and trustees all said in commenting on their relationships in fundraising, the first commitment is to the cause, the mission of the organization. Trustees' commitments to the cause are essential to success. Service to the organization inspires this commitment.

Staff members bring the same dedication to the cause. Staff must also inspire and manage the fundraising process through their competence. Working together and drawing on each other's strengths, trustees and staff form a mutually satisfying partnership that results in successful fundraising. This is the most rewarding outcome of such relationships because the process meets the needs of all those—trustees, staff, and donors—who serve the cause of the not-for-profit organization.

Conclusions and implications

Our interviews with persons in organizations that are successful in raising funds confirmed the importance of involving trustees in the process. The partnership relationships described by those we interviewed matched the working relationships proposed by Ilsley (1990).

Our review of published materials and our interviews also confirm the values of teamwork and division of labor as these apply to organized fundraising for nonprofit institutions. Our general conclusion is that organizations that raise funds successfully foster attitudes of trust and respect between board members and staff for their complementary resources and roles.

The implications for staff and trustee development are clear. Staff must be trained to understand the skills and strengths they bring to the trustee-staff team so that they can approach trustees with confidence. Staff training must also focus on the importance of providing leadership by example to trustees rather than by managing and directing them tightly. Training for trustees also should include an overview of the support and leadership they can expect from staff, with a focus on the special strengths that trustees bring to the fundraising process.

Based on our interviews, we believe that bringing trustees and staff together for common training sessions and for dialogue about their complementary roles is beneficial. We also believe that mentorship of junior staff by senior staff, to help prepare them to serve on trustee-staff fundraising teams, is important.

Both staff and trustees bring distinctive assets to the fundraising process: staff members' professional expertise and experience, and board members' peer relationships with prospects and their testimonials as committed donors. As they work together and succeed, both groups come to recognize and appreciate the importance of their mutual contributions.

Appendix A: Interview questions for staff (and executive director) on expectations of and interaction with trustees in the fundraising process

1. Do you (your staff members) work with trustees in the fundraising process?

2. What is the nature of your interaction (the interaction of your staff) with the trustees in the fundraising process?

3. Do you (your staff members) enjoy this experience? If so, why? If not, why?

4. Is there a written job description outlining trustee responsibilities in fundraising? If so, is it useful to you in this process? If not, should there be one, and what should it contain?

5. How would you describe the relationship between yourself (your staff) and the trustees in carrying out fundraising tasks?

6. Do you (your staff members) take a leadership role, provide direction and guidance, and initiate activity for trustees?

7. Do you provide follow-up, clerical and detail work, and other support requested? Which of the two groups of activities in questions 6 and 7 do you regard as the most important?

8. From your perspective, what are the professional skills that you (your staff members) bring to the fundraising process? Do these skills enable you (them) to play a leadership and directing role for trustees in the fundraising process?

9. How do you (your staff members) prepare yourself (themselves) to provide leadership and direction for trustees who may be from a more influential, affluent socioeconomic stratum than you (they) are?

10. Is there a written set of procedures that describe your (your staff's) relationship with trustees for fundraising? If so, how well does it cover the aspects you consider most important?

11. How would you describe the ideal relationship between yourself (a staff member) and trustees in the fundraising process? What aspects do you consider essential to success?

Appendix B: Interview questions for trustees on expectations of and interaction with staff and executive director in the fundraising process

1. Approximately how many nonprofit organizations do you serve as trustee?
2. For one or any of these organizations, do you solicit gifts as part of your trustee responsibility?
3. Do you enjoy this experience? If so, why? If not, why?
4. Is there a written job description outlining your responsibilities in fundraising? If so, is it useful to you in this process? If not, should there be one, and what should it contain?
5. Do you work with a fundraising staff member other than the CEO of the organization in carrying out your fundraising tasks? If yes, with whom do you work in the organization to carry out your fundraising tasks? Please describe the person's position.
6. How would you describe the relationship between yourself and the staff person in carrying out fundraising tasks?
7. Do you expect the staff member to take a leadership role, provide direction and guidance, and initiate activity on your behalf?
8. Do you rely on the staff person for follow-up, clerical and detail work, and other support you request? Which of the items in questions 7 and 8 do you regard as the most important activity?
9. From your perspective, what are the professional skills that the staff member with whom you work brings to the fundraising process? Do these skills allow the staff member to play a leadership and directing role for you in the fundraising process?
10. Are you able to permit yourself to be managed and directed by the staff person in the fundraising process? What tensions do you experience in this process?
11. Is there a written set of procedures that describes your relationship with the professional staff member? If so, how well does it cover the aspects you consider most important?

12. How would you describe the ideal relationship between your-self and a staff member in the fundraising process? What aspects do you consider essential to success?

References

Greenleaf, R. K. *Servant Leadership*. New York: Paulist Press, 1977.

Houle, C. O. *Governing Boards: Their Nature and Nurture*. San Francisco: Jossey-Bass, 1989.

Ilsley, P. J. *Enhancing the Volunteer Experience: New Insights on Strengthening Volunteer Participation, Learning, and Commitment*. San Francisco: Jossey-Bass, 1990.

Ingram, R. T. *Ten Basic Responsibilities of Nonprofit Boards*. National Center for Nonprofit Boards Governance Series, no. 1. Washington, D.C.: National Center for Nonprofit Boards, 1988.

O'Connell, B. *Fund Raising*. Washington, D.C.: INDEPENDENT SECTOR, 1987.

Rosso, H. A., and Associates. *Achieving Excellence in Fund Raising: A Comprehensive Guide to Principles, Strategies, and Methods*. San Francisco: Jossey-Bass, 1991.

TIMOTHY L. SEILER *is director of Operations of the Fund Raising School, Indiana University Center on Philanthropy. He is formerly vice president of Indiana University Foundation in charge of its Indianapolis office.*

EUGENE R. TEMPEL *is vice chancellor for external affairs at Indiana University-Purdue University, Indianapolis, and is also executive director of The Fund Raising School.*

A study of the effective utilization of the president, trustees, private citizens, and staff and faculty in the solicitation of major gifts is presented here. In different steps of the major-gift process, the relative importance of each of these four groups was found to change; moreover, these groups were influential with major-gift donor prospects both for the same and for different reasons.

6

In pursuit of major gifts: Nondevelopment personnel in fundraising

Walter R. "Win" Winfree III

THE SUCCESSFUL SOLICITATION of major gifts from private individuals is critical to college and university development programs. Success in these solicitations often involves the efforts of four groups of individuals who are not themselves members of an institution's development staff. These four groups are referred to in this chapter as nondevelopment personnel and include the president of the school, its board of trustees, private citizens who are friends of the institution, and nondevelopment staff and faculty.

In the study reported here, the efforts of each of these four groups were investigated through the four basic steps of the major-gift solicitation process: identification and rating (rating is the

NEW DIRECTIONS FOR PHILANTHROPIC FUNDRAISING, NO. 4, SUMMER 1994 © JOSSEY-BASS PUBLISHERS

process by which it is determined what size gift a potential donor might favorably consider), cultivation, in-person solicitation, and, finally, the thank-you process following the gift. The knowledge garnered from this study has been used to generate practical guidelines to help senior development officers effectively apply the time and skills of these four groups of individuals and thus, in turn, increase success in the acquisition of major gifts at their schools.

For the purposes of this study, the term *major gift* was defined as any gift of $100,000 or greater. The research population encompassed all accredited, degree-granting four-year colleges and universities in the United States that solicit major gifts from private individuals. The actual research sample involved collecting data from the chief development officer at each of the 223 schools that had received one or more gifts of $1 million or greater from private individuals as reported in *Giving USA, Philanthropic Digest*, or the *Chronicle of Higher Education* between January 1, 1985, and December 31, 1987.

The research instrument was a mailed questionnaire, which was sent to the chief development officer of the 223 schools in the research sample. Replies were received from 162 institutions for a response rate of 72.6 percent, which is exceptionally high for a mailed questionnaire and indicates the level of interest among questionnaire recipients in this study.

Examination of these data revealed, first, that nondevelopment personnel had played a significant role in the solicitation of over half of the major-gift dollars collected. In addition, analysis indicated that the president or chancellor was, overall, the most important advocate for an institution's development program, followed by the trustees, private citizens, and, finally, the nondevelopment staff and faculty, but that in different steps of the major-gift process the relative importance of each of these groups changed. In addition, it was determined that the services of the private citizens and nondevelopment staff and faculty groups were underutilized at a number of the schools.

Further examination of these data revealed specific reasons that each of the nondevelopment groups might be influential with major-donor prospects. It is of particular significance that the nondevelopment groups were found to be influential with major-donor prospects for different reasons, although some of the reasons were shared.

Research questions

QUESTION 1. *Do nondevelopment personnel commonly play a role in the major-gift solicitation process?*

The question was designed to determine the percentage of schools in which one or more of the four groups of nondevelopment personnel commonly play a significant role in some aspect of the major-gift solicitation process. For the 156 schools reporting on this variable, 93.6 percent (146) stated that nondevelopment personnel commonly played a significant role in some aspect of the major-gift process, and only 6.4 percent (10) of the schools reported that they did not.

Conclusion from question 1: Nondevelopment personnel are successfully utilized in the major-gift solicitation process at the vast majority of four-year colleges and universities in the United States.

QUESTION 2. *If nondevelopment personnel do not commonly play a significant role in some aspect of the major-gift solicitation process, why?*

As noted above, at ten of the schools reporting on this variable, the chief development officers responded that nondevelopment personnel were not used in the major-gift solicitation process. The top four reasons (reported as weighted percentage values) for this nonutilization were as follows: (1) lack of time and resources to train nondevelopment personnel (34 percent), (2) president, trustees, private citizens, or nondevelopment staff and faculty do not think that it is their responsibility to help in the major-gift solicitation process (20 percent), (3) president, trustees, private citizens, or nondevelopment staff and faculty do not like to help in the major-gift solicitation process (16 percent), and (4) unavailability of nondevelopment personnel (16 percent). The remaining reasons reported (14 percent) were "other."

Conclusions from question 2: Only ten schools (6.4 percent) fell into this research category, and thus some caution must be used when interpreting these data. Nonetheless, speculation can still be offered as to why nondevelopment personnel do not commonly play a significant role in the major-gift process at some schools. Possible explanations for nonutilization are (1) the presence of institutions at which the appointment as either president or as a trustee does not carry with it the responsibility for active participation in the major-gift solicitation process; (2) insufficient funding or a failure of budgetary or time management, or both, of the development office, resulting in a lack of resources for the long-term recruitment, cultivation, and training of nondevelopment personnel for the major-gift solicitation process; and (3) lack of understanding by leadership within either the development office or the institution at large as to the potential for success inherent to the use of nondevelopment personnel as a component of the major-gift solicitation process.

> QUESTION 3. *What percentage of total major-gift dollars were solicited with nondevelopment personnel having played a significant role in some aspect of the solicitation process?*

For the 144 schools reporting on this variable, 56.9 percent of the major-gift dollars were solicited with nondevelopment personnel having played a significant role in some aspect of the process. The remaining 43.1 percent of major-gift dollars were solicited with nondevelopment personnel *not* having played a significant role in the process. The data were also arranged by size of professional development staff, to see whether schools with larger or smaller staffs reported higher or lower percentages of major-gift dollars solicited with nondevelopment personnel playing a significant role. No discernible pattern was evident.

Conclusions from question 3: The efforts of nondevelopment personnel are of significance in the collection of over half of the major-gift dollars that come from private individuals. By inference, these data suggest that the efforts of nondevelopment personnel and of professional development staff are of approximately equal importance in the solicitation of these major-gift dollars. Further review of these data indicates that the significance of nondevelopment personnel in the solicitation of major-gift dollars does not vary based solely on the size of a particular school's development staff.

QUESTION *4. For the major-gift dollars solicited with significant involvement by nondevelopment personnel, what percentage of this success could be attributed to each of the four groups: president, trustees, private citizens, and nondevelopment staff and faculty?*

The results were as follows: (1) president, 40.5 percent; (2) trustees, 25.8 percent; (3) private citizens, 18.7 percent; and (4) nondevelopment staff and faculty, 15 percent.

Conclusions from question 4: The president is the single most important advocate for an institution's development efforts, the services of the trustees are next most important, and those of private citizens and nondevelopment staff and faculty groups are, respectively, third and fourth in importance. When answering question 4, some respondents placed a zero in one or more of the boxes, indicating that a group or groups of nondevelopment personnel was utilized but that no major-gift success could be attributed to their efforts. The results were as follows: (1) president, 0 percent; (2) trustees, 2.3 percent; (3) private citizens, 3.8 percent; and (4) nondevelopment staff and faculty, 4.4 percent. These results indicate that when the services of one or more of the groups of nondevelopment personnel are used, some major-gift success can almost always be attributable to their efforts.

For research question 4, respondents were also asked to place an X in the box if one or more of the four groups of nondevelopment personnel were not involved in the major-gift solicitation process at their schools, thus revealing information about schools that utilized some, but not all, of the four groups of nondevelopment personnel. The percentages for those schools reporting that some of their groups were not utilized were as follows: (1) president, 0.8 percent; (2) trustees, 6.2 percent; (3) private citizens, 24.1 percent; and (4) nondevelopment staff and faculty, 23 percent. Since results from an earlier part of question 4 showed that some major-gift success almost always occurred when the services of nondevelopment individuals were utilized, and this part of the question yielded the findings that at 24.1 percent of the schools private citizens and at 23 percent of the schools nondevelopment staff and faculty were not used, then it is clear that the services of these two groups were most probably being underutilized.

> QUESTION 5. *What are the top reasons that each group of so-licitors is influential with major-gift prospects?*

This research question contained a list of twenty-four possible reasons, including "other," that an individual might be *influential* with a major-donor prospect. This question was concerned with evaluating the relative importance attached to each of these determinants by the chief development officer when deciding which nondevelopment personnel to assign to work with each major-donor prospect. The top reasons that each of the four groups were deemed influential are presented in Table 6.1.

Conclusions from question 5: These data indicate that the senior development officers, for different nondevelopment groups, weighed specific determinants more or less heavily when deciding

Table 6.1. Most Frequently Cited Reasons That Nondevelopment
Personnel Were Viewed as Influential, by Group

Group	Reason Influential	Percentage of Respondents
Presidents		
	President of school	34.9
	Personally persuasive	16.4
	Highly knowledgeable about a specific project or program	14.8
	High personal stature or achievements	11.3
	Other	22.6
Trustees		
	Already made a major gift themselves	22.2
	Trustee of school	17.8
	Personal friend	12.5
	Other	47.5
Private Citizens		
	Already made a major gift themselves	21.6
	Personal friend	16.0
	Business acquaintance	12.1
	Other	50.3
Nondevelopment Staff and Faculty		
	Highly knowledgeable about a specific project or program	43.6
	Personally persuasive	17.4
	High personal stature or achievements	12.3
	Other	26.7

which individuals had the greatest likelihood of being influential with major-donor prospects. Notable among these determinants were the influence of the president simply because he or she was the president and the influence of the nondevelopment staff and faculty group as sources of expert information about specific projects or programs.

> QUESTION 6. *What are the top reasons, overall, that chief development officers perceive of nondevelopment personnel as influential?*

The data from all four groups of nondevelopment personnel were combined in order to give an overall view of the top reasons that chief development officers perceived nondevelopment personnel as influential. The results are presented in Table 6.2.

Conclusions from question 6: When data from all four groups of nondevelopment personnel were combined, the single determinant perceived as most important was that the nondevelopment representative is highly knowledgeable about a specific project or program. This finding was certainly due, in part, to the high score given this determinant for the staff and faculty group (see Table 6.1). However, this datum nonetheless underscores the importance of having nondevelopment representatives who are very well versed in the salient facts surrounding the project, program, or institution that they are representing.

This study breaks new ground with the finding that "being highly knowledgeable about a specific project or program" is, overall, the single most important reason that representatives might be influential with major-gift prospects. This finding is important because, in my opinion, many nondevelopment representatives are presently being sent forth to meet with major-gift prospects before they are thoroughly informed as to the specifics of the project or programs that they are representing.

The data in Table 6.2 also reveal that such determinants as net worth or wealth similar to that of the prospect, highly skillful in

Table 6.2. Overall Most Frequently Cited Reasons That Nondevelopment Personnel Were Viewed as Influential

Reason Influential	Percentage of Respondents
Highly knowledgeable about a specific project or program	14.7
Personally persuasive	12.8
President of school	11.2
Already made a major gift themselves	11.1
High personal stature or achievements	9.7
Personal friend	8.5
Business acquaintance	5.9
Trustee of school	5.2
Net worth or wealth similar to that of the prospect	3.9
Highly skillful in making the "ask"	3.3
Alumnus	2.8
Highly skillful in cultivating major-donor prospects	2.8
Sum of all other reasons	8.1

cultivating or making the ask, a fellow alumnus, and much experience in the major-gift solicitation process (the score for which was so low that it was combined into the "other" group) are, *as individual determinants*, of less importance in influencing major-donor prospects than is widely believed. Also of much importance is the fact that when the data were combined, no single determinant or group of determinants stood out as a key element or elements in influencing major-gift prospects. This finding underscores the importance of remembering that the manner in which one approaches, cultivates, solicits, thanks, and eventually recultivates a major donor must in each case be uniquely personalized.

QUESTION 7. *How important is each of the following four groups of nondevelopment personnel to each step in the major-gift solicitation process?*

This research question was concerned with determining the relative importance of each of the four groups of nondevelopment personnel to each of the four steps in the major-gift solicitation process. The results are presented in Table 6.3.

Conclusions from question 7: The president and trustee groups were, in general, viewed as most important in the various steps of the major-gift solicitation process. Exceptions to this finding are seen for the first step, identification and rating, where the services of the private citizen group were viewed as more important than those of the president group, and for the final step, the thank-you process, where the efforts of the nondevelopment staff and faculty group were seen to have higher than usual importance.

> QUESTION 8. *What is the overall importance of each group of nondevelopment personnel to the entire major-gift solicitation process?*

The overall importance of each group of nondevelopment personnel to the entire major-gift solicitation process was next examined. The results of these analyses were as follows: (1) president, 28 percent; (2) trustees, 26.2 percent; (3) private citizens, 23.7 percent; and (4) nondevelopment staff and faculty, 22.1 percent.

Conclusions from question 8: These findings substantiate the conclusions derived from the data for question 4 by again showing a sequence in which the president is seen as the most important advocate for an institution's development efforts, the trustees are of next importance, and the efforts of the private citizens and nondevelopment staff and faculty are, respectively, third and fourth in importance.

Final recommendations

First, the services of the president should be recognized as, potentially, the most important for an institution's development efforts, those of the trustees as next most important, and those of private citizens and nondevelopment staff and faculty as, respectively, third

Table 6.3. Importance of Nondevelopment Personnel to Each Step in the Major-Gift Solicitation Process, by Group

Step	Percentage of Respondents
Identification and Rating	
Private citizens	29.3
Trustees	29.0
Presidents	21.0
Nondevelopment staff and faculty	20.7
Cultivation	
Presidents	29.6
Trustees	25.7
Nondevelopment staff and faculty	23.0
Private citizens	21.7
In-Person Solicitation	
Presidents	29.8
Trustees	26.3
Private citizens	23.5
Nondevelopment staff and faculty	20.4
Thank You	
Presidents	31.2
Nondevelopment staff and faculty	24.5
Trustees	23.7
Private citizens	20.6

and fourth in importance. These levels of importance, generally speaking, hold true for all four steps of the major-gift solicitation process with the exceptions of the identification and rating step, where the services of private citizens are of special importance and those of presidents are of less importance, and for the thank-you step, where the efforts of nondevelopment staff and faculty are of higher than usual importance.

Second, with regard to schools that do not commonly use, or underutilize, the services of nondevelopment personnel in their major-gift process, more time, money, and resources should first be allocated for educating the various nondevelopment constituencies as to their responsibilities to help in the process, the potential impact of their involvement on the overall success of the major-gift effort, and the personal satisfaction and fulfillment that will probably result from their involvement. Once these nondevelopment personnel are involved and committed, more time, effort, and money should be allocated for the proper training and preparation of these individuals for their various development activities, so as to maximize the success of their efforts.

Third, to the extent that the services of private citizens and nondevelopment staff and faculty are, at a significant number of schools, underutilized, these two groups should be brought more actively into the major-gift solicitation process. The result will probably be increased success in major-gift dollars solicited.

Fourth, a senior development officer should, for different nondevelopment groups, weigh specific determinants more or less heavily when deciding which individuals have the greatest likelihood of influencing a major-donor prospect. Notable among these determinants are the influence of the president, simply because he or she is the president, and the influence of nondevelopment staff and faculty as sources of expert information about specific projects or programs. Moreover, since, in the present study, the determinant perceived as most important was that the nondevelopment representative should be highly knowledgeable about a specific project or program, it is important to have nondevelopment representatives who are very well versed in the salient facts surrounding the project, program, or institution that they are representing. In contrast, the determinants of net worth or wealth similar to that of the prospect, highly skillful in cultivating or making the ask, alumnus, and much experience in the major-gift solicitation process are, as individual determinants, of less importance in influencing major-donor prospects than is widely believed.

Also of much importance is the fact that when the data were combined (Table 6.2), no single determinant stood out as a key element in influencing major-gift prospects. This finding underscores the importance of personalizing each step of the major-gift solicitation process for each potential major donor.

Fifth, the data collected in this study did not lend themselves to a definitive statement regarding the percentage of major-gift success that could be directly attributed to the efforts of professional development staff versus the four groups of nondevelopment personnel. However, the responses to question 3 suggest that the efforts of nondevelopment personnel and of professional development staff may be of approximately equal importance in relation to the overall major-gift dollars collected.

Similarly, these data did not specifically address a comparison of the relative merits of using paid nondevelopment personnel, such as the president or nondevelopment administrators and faculty, versus nonpaid nondevelopment personnel such as trustees and private citizens. However, the data collected in response to questions 7 and 8 suggest that both of these groups are of great significance to the major-gift solicitation process. This comparison as well as that of the merits or demerits of using professional development staff versus the four groups of nondevelopment personnel warrant additional study and research.

Finally, based on the literature reviewed for this study and the study's data, colleges and universities are well advised to reallocate their resources to more effectively involve and utilize the services of their nondevelopment personnel. These investments will be far outweighed by the additional major-gift dollars collected.

WALTER R. "WIN" WINFREE III *is a consultant in development, headquartered in Hampton, Virginia. He is former executive campaign director for Community Counseling Service and has also worked with Ketchum, Inc., consulting both nationally and internationally.*

To govern or not to govern effectively, that is the question; one of the answers is to train not-for-profit board members appropriately.

7

Trustee education: Suggested curriculum for not-for-profit boards

Santo D. Marabella

Institutions need two kinds of leaders: those who are inside and carry the active day-to-day roles; and those who stand outside but are intimately concerned and who, with the benefit of some detachment, oversee the active leaders. These are the *trustees*.
—ROBERT K. GREENLEAF (1973)

AS NOT-FOR-PROFIT ORGANIZATIONS (NFPs) prepare for the numerous challenges of the twenty-first century, their need to have boards of directors or trustees composed of knowledgeable and competent voluntary leaders is more crucial to succeeding and surviving than ever.

For approximately the past thirty-five years, communities have recognized the importance of training those who serve as trustees and directors of local NFPs, with the emergence of community leadership programs (CLPs). These programs, among other functions, are training and educating individuals to be better board members.

One strategy to help CLPs determine the components of their training curriculum for building better boards is, first, to understand the scope and activities of the job of a board member. Once we

NEW DIRECTIONS FOR PHILANTHROPIC FUNDRAISING, NO. 4, SUMMER 1994 © JOSSEY-BASS PUBLISHERS

understand the scope and activities of the job of a board member, once we understand why board members exist and what it is they do, the components of such a curriculum become more evident.

In this discussion, I look, first, at the scope of a board member's job, or governance. Then I explore the activities in which board members engage. Finally, based on assumptions drawn from the discussion, I propose curriculum components for trustee education.

Background on boards

What are boards? Where did they come from? Why do they exist? Knowing the responses to these questions is helpful to conceptualizing what board members do. Below is a brief look at the evolution and purpose of boards.

Origin of boards

The citizen governing board is thought to be the first political structure ever created as a strategy to resolve conflict in a society moving beyond the small familial group (Greer, 1982). Houle (1989) described the evolution of boards to manage the growing complexities of societal development and to institutionalize individual effort. For these reasons, government boards—municipal councils, legislatures, and Congress—as well as boards with responsibilities for schools, health and welfare, and education institutions, to name a few, evolved. Houle viewed boards in the context of a tripartite system in which an organization's membership carries out the work, managed by an administrator and governed, through the establishment of policies, by a board.

It is estimated that there are more than 1,140,388 NFPs recognized by the Internal Revenue Service (IRS) as tax-exempt (Internal Revenue Service, 1992), which are required by law to appoint and maintain a board of directors (MacLeod, 1989). We can thus infer that there are approximately the same number of boards—over one million! The discussion here focuses on the board members of NFPs classified as "public regarding or charitable" (Van Til, 1988).

Board governance

Of concern here are members of governing boards that develop and determine policy and govern the affairs of NFPs, rather than manage them. Governance, the foundation for the board members' activities, is a dynamic concept too vast to discuss here except for three particularly relevant issues.

First, the days of board governance as a rubber stamp for the dominant executive director are gone (Bartlett and Grantham, 1980; Howell, 1979; Lear, 1989; Reiss, 1990). Those were the days when the major requirement from a board member was use of his or her name and a contribution of money. Bartlett and Grantham (1980) credit advancements in the mental health field in the 1960s and 1970s for strengthening citizen participation and ownership in public programs and beginning the process of erasing the "ink" of the rubber stamp.

Second, governance is usually not management. Dayton (1987) said that governance is seeing to it that the organization is well managed, rather than managing it oneself.

Third, in reviewing the literature it is apparent that, while there are many ways to conceptualize what it means to govern (Chait and Taylor, 1989; Dayton, 1987; Greer, 1982; MacLeod, 1989), there is general agreement that governance is central to the work of the boards of NFPs (American National Red Cross, 1979; Better Business Bureau of Eastern Pennsylvania, 1986; Chait and Taylor, 1989; Dayton, 1987; Fink, 1989; Greer, 1982; Houle, 1989; MacLeod, 1989; National Academy for Voluntarism, n.d.; O'Connell, 1985). Three themes are common to most definitions of governance: power, control, and influence (Cibulka, 1981; Dayton, 1987; Howell, 1979; Thain and Leighton, 1988; Zald, 1969). To govern, then, is to have and use power, control, and influence to perform what board members do (or need to be doing!).

Board activities

Boards do a lot of things. From the literature (American National Red Cross, 1979; Bartlett and Grantham, 1980; Better Business Bureau of Eastern Pennsylvania, 1986; Houle, 1989; MacLeod, 1989; National Academy for Voluntarism, n.d.; O'Connell, 1985; Oleck, 1980), a categorized list of board activities can be compiled:

Staff-related: appoint and support a chief staff officer or executive director, monitor the executive director's performance

Strategic planning: clarify the NFP's mission, determine its goals and objectives, develop or approve strategic plans or policies to achieve goals and objectives, preserve institutional independence

Program-related: develop programs and plans to implement the programs, monitor program operations

Resource-connecting: identify and develop resources, allocate resources, ensure financial solvency

Accountability: maintain legal, internal, and public accountability

Assessment: evaluate or assess the performance and effectiveness of the program, the board, and the organization

Staff-related activities are considered the primary and most important activities of a board (Houle, 1989; O'Connell, 1985). Hiring the executive director, and firing him or her if necessary, is critical. The executive director significantly impacts the board's ability to accomplish its goals and objectives because that person is the chief implementer for the board. The board activities in this area do not end with hiring the "right" person. The board must support, guide, and work with the executive director. Equally important, the board must assess the executive director's performance to ensure positive movement toward goal achievement and to prevent small problems from becoming larger, unmanageable ones.

The next major set of activities relates to strategic planning.

These activities help the board keep the organization in focus. The first step toward gaining (or keeping) focus is to clarify the NFP's mission. Many times boards will conduct retreats to create atmospheres that help them achieve focus. With a clearly articulated and broadly accepted mission, a board can set goals and develop plans and policies that not only preserve the NFP's independence but also move the NFP forward.

A board that performs strategic planning activities finds the work of program-related activities to be straightforward. The former activities usually result in an agenda for the kinds of programs that need to be explored or implemented. As is the case with the executive director, the board cannot stop with program development; the board must have a mechanism in place to monitor and observe the progress (or lack thereof) of its programs. This does not mean that the board operates the programs, but that it definitely needs to know how they are being implemented and what they are achieving.

The goal of resource-connecting activities is to provide the organization with the resources it needs not only to ensure financial solvency but also to fund the programs it wants to operate. Boards are asked to provide resources; not just money, but also contributions of time, expertise, and effort. Many times they loan or give supplies, equipment, support staff time, and expertise. Board members also provide resources through their contacts with various individuals or organizations and businesses in the community.

At other times, boards are asked to develop resources from internal means such as fundraising projects or to secure resources from outside sources such as foundations and businesses. In each instance, the board members "connect" community resources to meet organization needs.

In accountability activities (MacLeod, 1989; Oleck, 1980), the board has to perform a number of tasks that demonstrate that it answers to a variety of masters. This means that it accepts responsibility for its actions and has an obligation to prove that to various institutions or publics. First, there is legal accountability. The board must engage in various activities to be in compliance with the law.

For example, according to MacLeod (1989), the law requires a board to file articles of incorporation, to have bylaws that enumerate the duties and functions of the officers and the board, and to file various financial reports of income and expenses. Second, the board also engages in various activities that show its own organization that it is accountable. For example, in a NFP that has members, a board will issue an annual report to membership. Also, the NFP will provide in its bylaws for the opportunity of members to be elected to the board. Third, there are accountability activities directed toward the general public. The board drives the campaign to build and maintain positive community relations through projects or events that make the public aware of the NFP's existence and educate the public about its work. A good public image can avert unnecessary negative publicity in times of NFP crisis and can facilitate an NFP's effort to recruit volunteers or raise funds.

The final set of activities concern assessment. With competition for funding and volunteers at a high level (O'Connell, 1989), it is more important than ever that boards make sure that they, their programs, and their organizations are operating to maximize efficiency and effectiveness. Board, program, and organizational "audits" are performed internally to look at efficiency and effectiveness. Is the board, program, or organization doing what it is supposed to be doing and is it doing it well? In other cases, boards have outside professionals conduct program evaluations or board and organizational assessments.

Suggested curriculum components

How does a board member acquire the necessary power, influence, and control to govern and the skill and knowledge needed to perform the NFP board's duties? It could be said that some board members have "it" before they come on board. But these people seem to be the exceptions. If a NFP really wants its board members to govern, it needs to provide opportunities for them to do so.

The NFP, through its executive director, must provide the mechanisms to enhance a board member's ability to govern. But, in addition, education and training of board members via CLPs can be a complementary and effective way to help them fulfill their purpose and effectively engage in their board activities.

From this discussion about governance and board activities, which is informed by my experience in managing a CLP and researching NFP boards, a number of themes that seem critical to preparing persons for board service can be inferred:

Self-knowledge and awareness: First, prospective board members need to have insight about themselves—observing ego, as psychologists might put it. They need to know what talents, biases, and interests they bring with them to their board service. A training program that helps individuals identify these factors for themselves can be useful to board members as they strive to perform resource-connecting and assessment tasks.

Individual board members are selected because of the individual contributions they can make to the NFP. But a person's capabilities may not always be clear. Training programs that draw out the interests and skills of a board member and make them more obvious can be useful to the NFP, as well as to the individual. To the NFP and the board member, it is a way of focusing the board member's service to the NFP. The banker who has been selected to serve as a member of a board for his or her financial expertise, may express, upon some self-exploration, a desire to use her or his selling expertise (a less obvious skill) to call on community business leaders for the NFP's funding appeal.

Interpersonal relations: Second, prospective board members need to be able to communicate and work with other board members, especially those who have different styles of accomplishing tasks. They need to know how to approach others in a way that does not threaten but rather encourages input. These skills are especially useful in staff-related and resource-connecting activities.

The relationship between a board member who chairs the board of directors and the NFP's executive director is critical to a smooth operation. The ability to attain the executive director's cooperation in keeping the chair well-informed about developments in the NFP's operations, without threatening the professionalism or credibility of the executive director, contributes to the NFP's ability to thrive.

Community context: Third, a sense of the context of the community is important for board members. What issues are most relevant to this community, what resources most plentiful, and what role can they, and the NFP they represent, play in enhancing the quality of life in the community? This theme suggests the type of skills needed to perform accountability, program, assessment, and strategic planning tasks.

With so many NFPs, and so few community resources, the job of training the board member to assist the NFP in identifying and maintaining its strategic focus is important. Helping the NFP focus on its basic mission—the community need for which it was founded—and then working with staff in developing programs that pursue this mission will enable the NFP to sustain itself in these times of competition and limited resources.

Leadership skills: Fourth, what leadership skills are most appropriate and necessary to be effective as a board member in the NFP? How an individual puts it all together to make his or her voluntary leadership service as a board member meaningful to the NFP and the community can be summarized in her or his ability to lead as a board member. Strategic planning, staff-related, and assessment activities are relevant to this theme.

It takes strong leadership to fire the nonperforming executive director, to cut back or cut out the ineffective or unsuccessful program, and to alter the NFP's mission when the current one no longer serves its constituents. Governance is having and using the power, influence, and control needed to perform the duties of board members. It is the foundation of board service. Leadership skills, then, are concrete, practical tools for board members to employ in order to engage in these activities successfully.

These four themes suggest four corresponding components that any curriculum for training trustees and directors can include. The elements of the components are listed below:

Self-knowledge and awareness: ethics and values clarification, identification of personality type, personal leadership style established

Interpersonal relations: communication processes, conflict management, team building, and valuing individual and group diversity

Community context: accountabilities, liabilities, community issues and challenges, roles and responsibilities of voluntary leadership, community trusteeship

Leadership skills: board management, financial management, fundraising, marketing, needs assessment and organizational diagnosis, program development and evaluation, strategic planning

Implications

It is reasonable to assume that each of these themes as a component of a training curriculum can facilitate a board member's ability to govern. In other words, having self-knowledge and awareness, being a good communicator, understanding and valuing the community context, and possessing effective leadership skills can enable the board member to acquire the necessary power, influence, and control to effectively engage in the board activities described above. Some of the implications in practice for CLPs, NFPs, and board members are as follows.

For CLPs

Many models exist for operating CLPs. Some are issue-centered, which means their primary focus is to make participants aware and knowledgeable of community issues, problems, and strengths. Other models are project-centered and channel the participants' energies and efforts into planning and implementing a project that has a community impact or relevance (for example, development and implementation of an action plan to address, as a community, the psychosocial, economic, and health needs of persons with HIV or AIDS). In this type of model, the participants have an opportunity actually to do something for the community.

A third type of model combines the issue and project foci and adds a skills component, which typically is targeted toward enhancing the participants' leadership skills. Many times, programs that follow this model find it difficult to present leadership skills without anchoring them toward a particular type of leadership. In Leadership Berks, a CLP in Reading, Pennsylvania, with which I have worked for the past ten years, our leadership skills are grounded in those skills that help build board member effectiveness.

It is important for all CLPs to consider incorporating, in some way, a skills component that addresses the development of skills relevant to board member activities. Many participants of CLPs become involved in community organizations and NFPs as board or committee members. Enhancement of a participant's skills in board member activities not only would be a valuable and needed aspect of the participant's development as a community leader, in addition to knowing the community's issues and seeing a project through to completion, but also would seem to be an integral role for the CLP.

For NFPs

There are at least two implications for NFPs to consider. First, it would be appropriate for skills training in board member activities to be a part of each new board member's orientation. (This assumes, of course, that each new board member receives an orientation!) It is the responsibility of the NFP to ensure that each new board member (as well as existing ones) understands and agrees to the NFP's expectations of board members. Among the NFP's expectations is the performance of duties such as described in this chapter. Having a training component in new-member orientation programs could help the board member understand the NFP's expectations.

The second implication, an extension of the first, is that it may be helpful from time to time to schedule in-service training for *all* board members—new and veterans alike. NFPs and their boards are more accustomed to participating in board planning retreats, as their corporate counterparts have been doing. This type of skills training would more likely be accepted by the NFP board today than was previously the case.

For board members

There is one critical implication for board members to address here. Board members, today more than ever, are responsible for being responsible board members. Whether it concerns their fiduciary role in decision making or their liability for the board's and the organization's actions, NFP board members today, and from now on, must take the initiative to understand their role, to be knowledgeable about the organization's work, and to be aware of the impact, adverse or positive, of its actions on clients, volunteers, and the community at large. In other words, board members must take responsibility for knowing what they do not know, or finding out what they need to do. This means that board members must ask for training or information or guidance—from the executive director, the NFP, or the community—in order to perform their tasks in a conscientious and effective way.

NFPs that take these components into consideration when they design trustee education programs can provide vehicles for addressing issues and developing skills that are most pertinent to effective board membership. Then, there are two challenges for CLPs, NFPs and board members. First, they need to work together to ensure that board members are educated. Second, self-knowledge and awareness, interpersonal relations, and community context and leadership skills, at minimum, must constitute the focus of their education.

References

American National Red Cross. *The Work of a Chapter Board: A Guide for Chapter Board Members.* Washington, D.C.: American Red Cross, 1979.

Bartlett, D. P., and Grantham, R. J. "An Orientation and Training Program for Citizen Boards." *Administration in Mental Health*, 1980, *8* (2), 103–112.

Better Business Bureau of Eastern Pennsylvania. *The Responsibilities of a Nonprofit Organization's Volunteer Board.* Arlington, Va.: Council of Better Business Bureaus, 1986.

Chait, R. P., and Taylor, B. E. "Charting the Territory of Nonprofit Boards." *Harvard Business Review,* 1989, *67* (1), 44–54.

Cibulka, J. G. "Citizen Participation in the Governance of Mental Health Centers." *Community Mental Health Journal,* 1981, *17* (1), 19–36.

Dayton, K. N. *Governance Is Governance.* Washington, D.C.: INDEPENDENT SECTOR, 1987.

Fink, J. "Community Agency Boards of Directors: Viability and Vestigiality, Substance, and Symbol." In R. D. Herman and J. Van Til (eds.), *Nonprofit Boards of Directors: Analyses and Applications.* New Brunswick, N.J.: Transaction, 1989.

Greenleaf, R. K. *The Servant as Leader.* Newton Center, Mass.: Robert K. Greenleaf Center, 1973.

Greer, S. "Citizens' Voluntary Governing Boards: Waiting for the Quorum." *Policy Sciences,* 1982, *14,* 165–178.

Houle, C. O. *Governing Boards: Their Nature and Nurture.* San Francisco: Jossey-Bass, 1989.

Howell, S. P., Jr. "Training for Citizen Governance in Community Mental Health: A Proposed Model." *Administration in Mental Health,* 1979, *6* (3), 240–250.

Internal Revenue Service. *Annual Report.* Publication No. 55. Washington, D.C.: Government Printing Office, 1992.

Lear, R. W. "Evolving the Effective Board." *Chief Executive,* Jan.–Feb. 1989, p. 10.

MacLeod, B. V. "The Nonprofit Board of Directors." In L. E. Miller (ed.), *Managing Human Service Organizations.* Westport, Conn.: Quorum, 1989.

National Academy for Voluntarism. *The Board and Its Responsibilities.* Prepared for the United Way Volunteer Leadership Development Program. Battle Creek, Mich.: W. K. Kellogg Foundation, n.d.

O'Connell, B. *The Board Member's Book: Making a Difference in Voluntary Organizations.* New York: Foundation Center, 1985.

O'Connell, B. "Two Million Points of Light." *Across the Board,* 1989, *26* (3), 11–15.

Oleck, H. L. *Nonprofit Corporations, Organizations, and Associations.* (3rd ed.) Englewood Cliffs, N.J.: Prentice Hall, 1980.

Reiss, A. H. "Bottom Line: A Working Board of Directors." *Management Review,* 1990, *79,* 37–38.

Thain, D. H., and Leighton, D.S.R. "The Board of Directors: Key to Effective Governance." *Business Quarterly,* Spring 1988, pp. 77–80.

Van Til, J. *Mapping the Third Sector: Voluntarism in a Changing Social Economy.* New York: Foundation Center, 1988.

Zald, M. N. "The Power and Functions of Boards and Directors: A Theoretical Synthesis." *American Journal of Sociology*, 1969, 75, 97–111.

SANTO D. MARABELLA, M.B.A., D.S.W., *is assistant professor of management at Moravian College, Bethlehem, Pennsylvania, where he teaches courses in management, human resources, and policy and strategy. He also serves as executive director of Leadership Berks, a community leadership development program in Reading, Pennsylvania, and is chair of the Berks County Housing Authority. In addition, he provides consulting and training to arts, public housing, and social services boards on a regional and national level.*

Editor's Conclusion

ROOTED IN HISTORY, anchored in community responsiveness, and buoyed by shared vision, trusteeship provides countless benefits to those who do it and to the communities who enjoy its results. Those benefits, so well described in the diverse chapters of this volume, are the essential underpinning of democratized philanthropy: the belief that philanthropy is no longer the purview of the wealthy who give money but the right and responsibility of all who would give, ask, join, or serve. Words like *quality, access, excellence, account-ability, commitment,* and *vision* thread their way through many of the chapters here. These words define common expectations and common findings among the authors.

The word that lingers, however, after reading these chapters is one not explicitly mentioned in every chapter, though it is implic-it in each. That word is *partnership*. If there is one great lesson to be derived from these diverse studies and experiences, from this wide range of authors and commentaries, it is that the most suc-cessful fundraising campaigns and the most effective organizations depend on partnership.

This partnership has, at its root, a shared vision about the im-portance of meeting a critical community need: educational, health, social, cultural, religious, or whatever. It is the recognition of this need that should motivate and encourage people to serve on a board and keep an organization healthy. Trusteeship is not for the sake of the organization: It is for the well-being of the community.

This comprehensive and shared institutional vision marks and guides the partnership. It is communicated to the trustees by a staff who model leadership to a board. It is embraced, refined, tested, and acted on by trustees who are eager to know what is expected of them and everything they can about the organization. To effect such a partnership, roles and relationships must be well defined and communicated.

The partnership is continued and expanded through regular opportunities for honest and substantive communication, and it is reinforced most profoundly by mutual trust based on that communication. The partnership results in power that is positively exercised on behalf of the institution. And when the power balance tips unhealthily toward either board or staff, it is essential that trustees and staff work together to identify and solve the problem so that balance can be restored.

Trustees influence the fundraising success of an organization both directly and indirectly. While the reluctance of board members to fundraise continues to trouble the sector, there are opportunities for even the most reluctant trustee to contribute to the fundraising process. Organizations must recognize these opportunities and work with trustees to ease their comfort level as they develop relationships with new or known community members that could result in generous gifts to the organization.

Professionals should be concerned that their trustees are well informed, inspired, enthused, and willing to be articulate conversationalists about the organization on whose board they serve and the mission it is fulfilling. This willingness to tell the story, to engage others in an understanding of the broader mission, and to participate in events and opportunities that bring people closer to the mission or the organization can move trustees into a powerful partnership with the organization that will increase their comfort with fundraising.

Trustee apprehensiveness about fundraising has complex origins, many of which were covered in these chapters. As part of the teamwork that characterizes a power partnership between board and staff, diligent efforts must be undertaken by staff members and those on the board who are comfortable making the ask. They must, through their example, provide ways in which those who are fearful of asking can participate in a solicitation or become involved in relationship building.

The rich source references provided in many of the chapters can lead to a deeper understanding among those who read this journal. The sources also can serve as appropriate lists of materials for staff members to encourage their boards to read.

Fundraising is not the only responsibility of boards, and these chapters address well their other tasks or functions. Experience with numerous organizations leads to the riveting conclusion that these other activities should not subsume fundraising, but they must be attended to if fundraising is going to be done easily and confidently. The internal issues of budgeting, legal compliance, hiring or firing the executive director, and making certain facilities and program decisions in conjunction with the staff are functions that are and should be so systematized and internalized by boards—and so well managed at the procedural level by staff—that they do not detract from the trustee's role as asker and advocate in the community.

Not-for-profit organizations are unique in their utilization of purely volunteer assistance. Daily, we are able to engage people who, without compensation, spend hours and days on behalf of organizations in which they deeply believe.

The not-for-profit sector depends on empowered trustees acting on behalf of community-based organizations. For that empowerment to occur, partnerships must be in place. These partnerships are built and sustained on mutual respect and understanding about the roles and responsibilities of staff and volunteers.

The chapters in this volume widen and deepen our understanding of the potential for involvement, empowerment, and partnership. They alert us to the possibilities to make our sector ever stronger.

Kay Sprinkel Grace
Editor

KAY SPRINKEL GRACE *is a San Francisco-based organizational consultant who provides workshops and consultation on issues related to leadership of the fundraising process. She is also on the faculty of The Fund Raising School, Indiana University Center on Philanthropy.*

Index

Ordering Information

NEW DIRECTIONS FOR PHILANTHROPIC FUNDRAISING is published quarterly in Fall, Winter, Spring, and Summer and available for purchase by subscription and individually.

SUBSCRIPTIONS for 1993–94 cost $59.00 for individuals (a savings of 35 percent over single-copy prices) and $79.00 for institutions, agencies, and libraries. Please do not send institutional checks for personal subscriptions. Standing orders are accepted.

SINGLE COPIES cost $19.95 when payment accompanies order. (California, New Jersey, New York, and Washington, D.C., residents please include appropriate sales tax.) Billed orders will be charged postage and handling.

DISCOUNTS for quantity orders are available. Please write to the address below for information.

ALL ORDERS must include either the name of an individual or an official purchase order number. Please submit your order as follows:
  Subscriptions: specify series and year subscription is to begin
  Single copies: include individual title code (such as PF1)

MAIL ALL ORDERS TO:
  Jossey-Bass Publishers
  350 Sansome Street
  San Francisco, California 94104-1310

FOR SUBSCRIPTION SALES OUTSIDE OF THE UNITED STATES, contact any international subscription agency or Jossey-Bass directly.